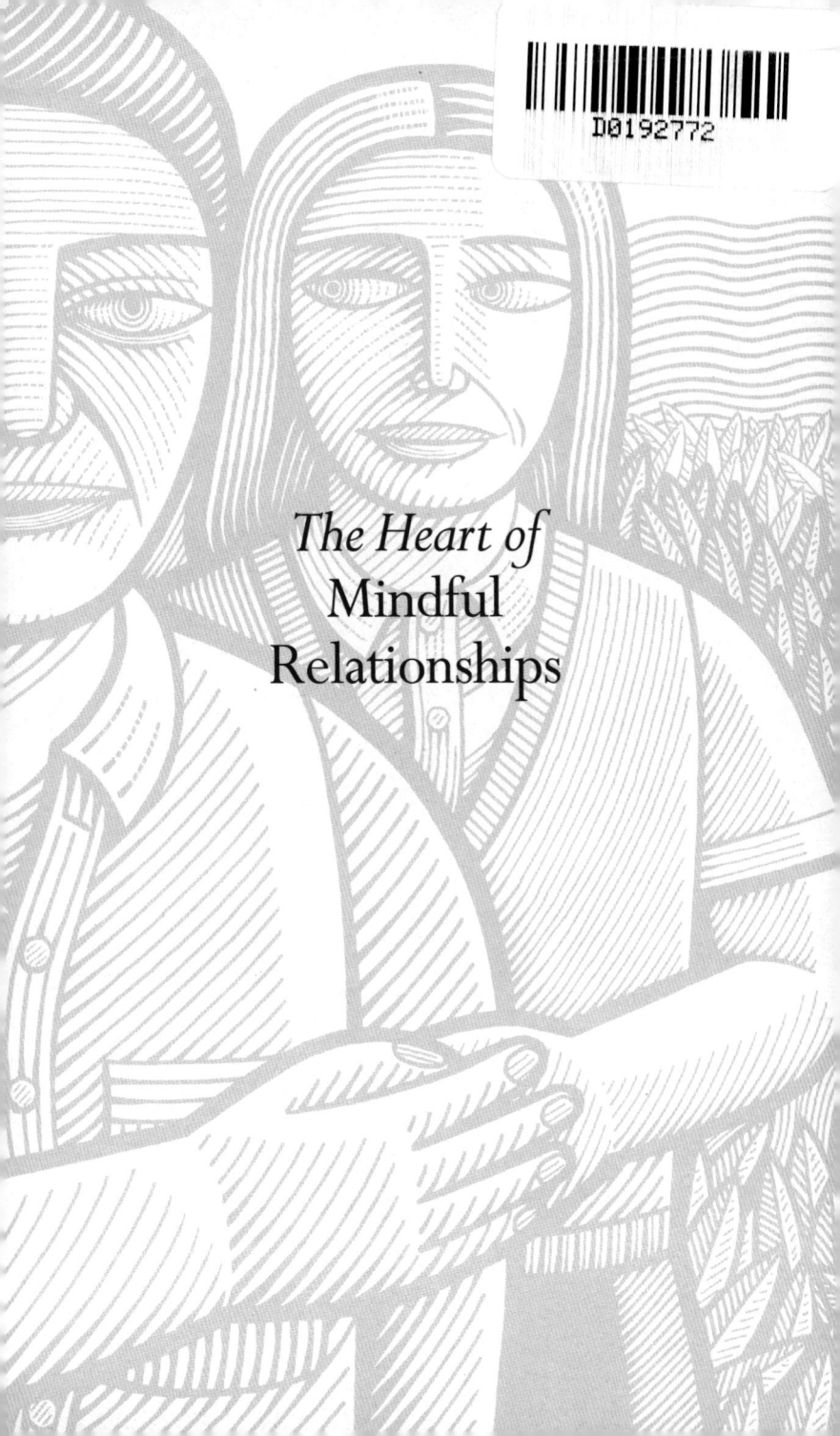

The Heart of
Mindful
Relationships

The Heart of Mindful Relationships

Meditations on Togetherness

Maria Arpa

Leaping Hare Press

First published in the UK in 2012 by

Leaping Hare Press

210 High Street, Lewes
East Sussex BN7 2NS, UK
www.leapingharepress.co.uk

ISBN: 978-1-908005-29-8

This book was conceived, designed and produced by

Leaping Hare Press

Creative Director PETER BRIDGEWATER
Publisher SOPHIE COLLINS
Commissioning Editor MONICA PERDONI
Art Director WAYNE BLADES
Senior Editor JAYNE ANSELL
Designer RICHARD CONSTABLE
Illustrator CLIFFORD HARPER

Printed in China
Colour Origination by Ivy Press Reprographics

10 9 8 7 6 5 4 3 2 1

CONTENTS

Acknowledgements 6

Introduction 7

CHAPTER ONE
Changing Your Relationship 12

CHAPTER TWO
Knowing Yourself 34

CHAPTER THREE
Receiving Your Partner 58

CHAPTER FOUR
The Task Ahead 80

CHAPTER FIVE
Authentic Dialogue 96

CHAPTER SIX
The Way Forward 118

CHAPTER SEVEN
Maintenance 130

A Relationship Contract 140

Index 142

Acknowledgements

◆

I would like to give gratitude to my two children, Rosy and Sam, who have helped me learn some important lessons about love, my partner David who unfailingly supports our joint vision, my brother Joseph who just accepts me the way I am, Dr Marshall Rosenberg who said some things that changed every aspect of my life and all the clients, participants and trainees who have trusted me to be a part of their lives.

INTRODUCTION

*Have you found yourself wondering
why some conversations with your partner end
unsatisfactorily, or why your partner doesn't cooperate?
Do you wish that communication between you and
your partner could be more agreeable and enjoyable?
The trouble is, if you keep doing things the same old
way, you cannot expect things to change for the better.
If you believe you have tried everything to
change things without success, now is the
time to try a new approach.*

ON BEING ONE HALF OF A COUPLE

◆

Being in an intimate relationship is a choice. How we conduct ourselves in that relationship is a responsibility. Achieving a happy state of shared togetherness is a dance that depends on both individuals continuously collaborating and adapting to find a harmonious rhythm. All the time spent learning and practising comes with no guarantees, yet many of us pursue the idea of a 'happy-ever-after' ending without truly considering the task or the process.

I BEGAN WRITING THIS BOOK ON A SATURDAY. It was unusual for me to work on a weekend, but David, my partner, had booked himself onto a life drawing class and that Saturday was the first of ten weekly classes, and this had created a space for me to write. However, there was a problem. We had made an agreement that weekends would be our 'couple' time. For me, it was an important agreement because during the week we often default to discussing work; we run a charity together and our work as mediators is both challenging and absorbing. We often divide up tasks and do things separately, so some days we don't see much of each other. Weekends are a time for strengthening our connection.

Of course, an agreement is not a rule. Flexibility is integral. Agreements are not cast in stone; they are open to renegotiation. So why am I irritated by him breezing off to his first class? After all, he is going to do something he enjoys; he will benefit

from it and I will benefit indirectly from this. Had we discussed it, I probably would have agreed that this was a good thing to do.

However, I was annoyed because he hadn't acknowledged our agreement and because I wasn't able to communicate my feelings in a satisfactory way. But did I want him to cancel his lesson? No, I didn't want my feelings to be the reason for him missing the class. What I really wanted was for him to be mindful of the choices he had made. His failure to do so had triggered my discomfort.

At the same time, I know that David can provide examples of my behaviours or actions that trigger discomfort in him. However, the fulfilment of our relationship lies in the quality of our communication, which means that we can discuss the things we don't like without fighting.

Having two divorces behind me, I have struggled to find a fulfilling relationship; I found myself in senseless arguments that only ever seemed to create more distance. However, as my work evolved from Counsellor to Reiki Master to Mediator and Trainer, I needed to find congruence between my personal and professional lives in order to be truly authentic in what I do. So when David and I got together we agreed that authenticity in the relationship was going to be our priority. We are both headstrong people so the realization that when we are in conflict we are both looking into a mirror has led to some deep research and provided some intensive learning. It is my intention to share our learning through this book.

Making a Relationship Work

Finding a partner is one of life's greatest gifts. When we find the love of our life, we embark on the relationship with great hope for our future happiness. We behave at our best and we make compromises in order to please our partner. We invest heavily in the relationship. We do all this in the hope of finding contentment, harmony and mutuality.

But sometimes it doesn't go to plan and many relationships fail to live up to our expectations. We argue, sulk, get revenge and stop talking to each other only to find ourselves in yet another unhappy impasse and, even worse, we find ourselves compromising on what we really want because we tell ourselves it is the only way to get some peace.

This book can help those embarking on a new relationship, those in a relationship that is stuck and those who simply wish to improve the quality of a relationship, by looking at how mindfulness can address issues in our own and our partner's lives. The main purpose of this book is to contribute to harmony in our relationships and reduce the amount of suffering we are all so capable of inflicting.

What is Mindfulness?

Mindfulness is a conscious awareness of the present moment – a recognition of reality in a situation, if you will. Mindfulness is a 'waking up' process. It asks us to live consciously, having regard for our sensations, feelings, thoughts and actions. This leads to

self-responsibility, which in a relationship leads to power sharing, equality and trust.

Mindfulness promotes and respects individuality and mutuality within the relationship and helps each couple find their own unique 'coupledom'. This is hard because we never get taught 'how to'; we just imagine it will 'come together'. As an individual, this process requires us to continuously review our *modus operandi*. In a relationship, there is another person to consider in parallel and in collaboration with our own process.

Fulfilment in a relationship is a journey rather than a destination and this book is a companion on that journey.

Working Through this Book

I would suggest that you first read the book to get a sense of the timescales involved in working through the processes. Then decide how and when it will suit you to work through them before beginning in earnest. The book contains a series of exercises that will take you out of your comfort zone and challenge you. You can work through them together or on your own, but if you decide to work alone then you are taking on the role of leading the change. There is nothing wrong with this, but you need to bear in mind that it is your job to engage your partner in such a way that they will want to join in.

The first two chapters are your individual groundwork, so let your partner know that you are embarking on a process that will begin with some time out for self-reflection.

CHAPTER ONE

CHANGING YOUR RELATIONSHIP

*Changing the way your relationship operates
is a process. It begins with a period of reflection
about how the relationship reached the point where
it needed changing and an understanding of how
the development of the relationship affected your
feelings, which in turn affected your contribution
to the partnership. The journey starts with your
personal positioning and how you arrived there.
With this knowledge you can begin some
self-healing and self-energizing.*

MAKING THE CHANGE

◆

Change in a relationship is a transformation or modification. You may be single and about to commit to a relationship, or you may already be in a relationship and want to leave it, or you may want to continue it under different terms or agreements. If you simply want to improve an already happy relationship, then you also want change. Let's prepare for that change.

To change something, you will have a greater chance of success if you know what it is you are changing from and what you want to change to.

So, what is the current state of your relationship? It is important to establish the starting point. If you didn't agree a framework for the relationship and it just sort of evolved, then you might have more work to do in establishing how you both see the relationship. In fact, you might be experiencing the relationship quite differently, so charging in with a list of demands or requests might be incomprehensible to your partner.

The first step is to understand how you experience the relationship and then to find out how your partner experiences it. This is your groundwork before you start communicating with each other in a new way. It is better if you work through this process of discovery on your own because you are trying to do your individual work first. Here are some questions you might find helpful:

- *What do I think about the relationship?*
- *When I think about my partner, what do I feel and sense?*
- *What do I harbour that is negative about the relationship?*
- *What do I harbour that is positive about the relationship?*
- *If I were asked to describe the relationship, what would I say?*

Now, I'd like you to carefully consider the current state of your relationship:

- *How do we each behave in this relationship?*
- *How do we make decisions?*
- *How do we agree things?*
- *How do we take each other into account?*
- *How do I look after myself?*
- *How do I care for my partner?*

These are not questions that can be answered instantly. Your first answer is usually just a reaction rather than a real response and so these are questions that require pondering and reflection. If the questions cause resistance or discomfort, acknowledge it and continue to reflect. This is only happening because you are not used to this level of examination and because they threaten to expose you to some of your less favourable traits or to an outcome you don't want to consider.

If you find yourself starting to blame and judge either yourself or your partner, stop the exercise and ask your subconscious to reflect on these questions. Simply put the questions to the back of your thoughts and ask your mind's computer to sort them out. Then, get on with your day and

come back to the questions later and try again. The feelings of blame and judgement you might be experiencing are merely defences against your discomfort.

If, after a few goes, you still find yourself generating judgements or blame in response to the questions, you will need to start from a different place. A good way of recognizing this is to notice if your responses are about you, or if they become about your partner's negative attitude or behaviour. In this case, ask yourself what has hurt you so much in this relationship or in other parts of your life that keep you in this place? Now try to work with the answers. Remember, the purpose of this self-examination is to understand the status quo.

• *What has the other person done?* You will need to be very specific about their actions. A general answer, such as 'failing to show me consideration' or 'being rude to me', will not suffice. It needs to be precise, such as 'allowing my birthday to pass without acknowledging it', or 'raising their voice and labelling me as selfish when I missed an appointment'. To work, it has be a specific action that could be recorded on a camcorder and shown to others.

• *How did I contribute to that person's actions?* Try to be as honest as you can. In any relationship the outcomes are a result of the contributory actions of all the parties involved. This doesn't mean that you are responsible for outcomes that are instigated by the other person; it means recognizing a series of events in which you were involved that led to

an outcome. Common contributions might include allowing frustration to build before saying something or expecting the other person to be a mind reader and know what you expect.

• *Did my part in it stem from my own emotional baggage?* Again, being honest and owning your part in it will contribute to learning about yourself which, in turn, helps you create the starting point for things that you would like to change. Your part in it could be never having dealt with a source of irritation that predates the relationship, such as feelings of betrayal or disappointment; or it could be a source of stress from outside the relationship – such as a difficult work situation – that you are bringing to the relationship.

• *What could I have done differently?* This is a tricky one because everything is easier with the benefit of hindsight. The aim is to use past events as learning for the present. Do this as a regular practice to develop a sense of awareness about how situations are influenced by what you said or did at the time.

• *Who am I really upset with?* It is really easy to blame others because this keeps everything at a safe distance where you have no power or control until the other person decides to change. You must consider your hurt and upset feelings for what they are rather than converting them into blame.

Understanding Resistance to Change

I am reminded of a separated couple – we'll call them Jude and Don – who came to see me to help resolve contact issues with their children. The hostility between them was so great that it was having noticeable psychological effects on their children. Jude had been subjected to emotional abuse in what was a volatile marriage and her hurt was so deep that she could not see past blaming Don. I asked the question of both of them: 'What could you have done differently?'

Interestingly, Don responded that he could have agreed to a divorce much earlier on and that there would have been less suffering if he hadn't insisted on trying to save the marriage. Jude responded that she could not have done anything differently. In her opinion, she had done everything correctly and he was totally to blame for her position. She resisted the idea that she could have said or done anything differently.

With that perspective, it was difficult to see how any progress could be made. She had invested in holding onto blame and seeking for him to be punished. I am not judging that position. We can hold any position we choose. The important thing is to acknowledge it and recognize how it affects our life in the present. In this case it was affecting the children, and her continued refusal to go beyond blame and punishment prevented her from finding any happiness in the present. When we hold onto blame and punishment, we continue to allow the past to affect the present.

Blame & Punishment

Mainstream Western society is based on a system of domination. This includes moralistic judgements of right or wrong and good or bad. It relies on there being an authority (someone who sets themselves up to know better) to set the bar for right and wrong with the expectation that people will obey. The system then motivates us to perform by using punishment and reward to get the behaviour it wants, and when things go wrong, it looks to marginalize the disobedient and diagnose what's wrong with them. The disobedient then lose all voice within the system so they shout louder and take more drastic action in order to get heard.

I see this system repeated in families. One couple I know wanted their children to behave in very set ways, which the children did not agree with. To get compliance, the parents stopped their children's allowances, grounded them, took away their mobile phones and continued punishing them until they agreed. Each child left home at the earliest possible opportunity, breaking free of the enforced rules, and the family structure broke down. In attempting to orchestrate a family, the parents had actually destroyed it.

We need to ask ourselves a simple question: What is more important in order for humans to flourish? Is it conformity or is it connection?

How Resistance Manifests Itself

If you are still having difficulty reflecting, think about resistance. Resistance manifests itself in many ways, which include:

- DISTRACTION – filling the space with something other than the topic.
- DISTANCING – moving away from the topic for change.
- DISMISSIVENESS – reducing or denying the topic.
- SUBVERSIVENESS – sabotaging or undermining the change process.
- AGGRESSION – forcing the change to stop.
- PASSIVITY – refusing to engage in the change process.

There are many reasons why a person can be resistant to self-examination, but they all stem from the person's level of readiness to change something. Reasons for resistance include:

- The risk associated with change being perceived as greater than the risk of staying the same.
- Not wanting to be different from people who want to keep things the same.
- Having no role model for the change.
- Fear of failure.
- A sense of being overwhelmed and overburdened.
- Believing that the change will undermine who we are.

It is worth exploring and understanding resistance if you are having trouble with this chapter and also if you are reading this book on your own. When you understand resistance it is easier to work through.

QUEST FOR CHANGE

◆

If you have spent time reflecting on all the questions in this chapter, you should now have a picture of where you are in this quest for change. The idea is that you have a clear and honest picture of how your relationship operates and how you both behave in it. By the end of this section you should be able to come up with a statement that reflects your position within the relationship.

THE WAY YOU BOTH OPERATE has created a 'system' and within that system you will have formed a 'position', which is a particular viewpoint from which you speak and act. Your partner is doing the same. Positions are not always as obvious as agreeing or disagreeing. They can be much more subtle in supporting beliefs and principles that you carried into the relationship from other life experiences. So what you say and do will reflect your position. You may well choose friends and pastimes that support your position, such as forming single-gender gossip clubs, which vilify the other sex.

And it can be much subtler than that. The choice of a single word can vastly alter the meaning of a conversation by how that word positions a situation. For example, saying, 'We've run out of milk' or 'Would you like me to get some milk?', suggests an entirely different position to, 'You've used up all the milk'. The words we use do not just describe a reality; they affect that reality.

Describing a Position in a Relationship

Now I'd like you to consider your position and further examine what this says about you. For example, I would describe my position in my relationship as: 'Very focused on what I want to achieve, while being equally open to having my views changed through meaningful dialogue. At the same time, I actively oppose all forms of emotional blackmail or manipulation and in those circumstances I don't take prisoners.'

I am not happy or unhappy about my position; nor do I think it is good or bad. It just is. Some parts of it serve me better than others and therefore I might choose to work on the areas that don't serve me well in order to increase joy in my life. What it tells my friends and family is that they had better be ready and willing to collaborate through meaningful dialogue or they will get very short shrift. When you put that in the context of my work as a facilitator, I am giving a strong message that I do not want to be cast in the role of facilitator in my down time. And if that role is being asked of me, then I expect to hear a clear request. Am I happy with that? Mostly. What about the parts that aren't covered by 'mostly'? Do I want to change them? Not enough to do anything about it; I am OK.

Now reflect on your own position. See if you can come up with a position statement in the same way I have. If you find it a struggle to do so, just remember that this could be a fear of exposure of not being good enough, either at this exercise or in a relationship or both.

OUR FEELINGS

◆

The next task is to go beyond our thoughts and into our feelings. By concentrating on our feelings we begin to release ourselves from the position we have created. I'm not suggesting we will abandon this position; but we can explore how we can go beyond the positions that inevitably limit us and reduce our capacity to change.

THE ABILITY TO FEEL is an extremely important part of being alive, and it is very useful to define and pinpoint how we are feeling in any given moment. Below are lists of words that make up a spectrum of feelings, such as anger or sadness. The list is not exhaustive so you might add to it with words of your own.

Read through the words and make a note of any that resonate for you when you think about your relationship.

ANGER Fury, outrage, annoyance, irritation, violence, frustration, powerlessness, hostility, hatred, exasperation, petulance, bitterness, rage.

SADNESS Grief, sorrow, gloom, misery, despair, depression, disappointment, despondency, loneliness.

FEAR Anxiety, uneasiness, apprehension, reluctance, alarm, vulnerability, panic.

SURPRISE Shock, astonishment, daze, awe, bewilderment, distress, amazement.

HURT Pain, anguish, agony, torment.

23

CONFUSION Worry, complacency, perplexity, anxiety, disorientation, puzzlement, turbulence.

DISGUST Contempt, scorn, disdain, revulsion, coldness, aversion, loathing, repugnance.

SHAME Guilt, embarrassment, regret, remorse.

FATIGUE Discouragement, depression, weariness, boredom, exhaustion, tiredness, heaviness.

CALM Serenity, balance, peace, relaxation, composure, detachment, contentment, stillness, radiance.

ENJOYMENT Happiness, joy, pride, pleasure, satisfaction, comfort, jubilance, amusement.

LOVE Acceptance, trust, affection, warmth.

INTEREST Curiosity, arousal, fascination, enthusiasm, liveliness, intrigue, enchantment.

ENERGY Excitement, elation, adventure.

OPENNESS Receptiveness, sensitivity.

*The ability to feel
is an extremely important
part of being alive.*

SELF-HEALING & SELF-ENERGIZING EXERCISE

◆

Now I'd like you to connect with any negative feelings that resonated for you in the previous exercise and begin the practice of self-healing. The following exercise requires you to use your imagination. It is important that you trust that the act of imagining makes it real for this exercise.

Y OU WILL NEED TO FIND A QUIET, safe, comfortable space to do this exercise, but it could be anywhere you feel happy. It is helpful if you are sure you won't be disturbed and you are clear of all urgent tasks for about 20 minutes.

1. Sit comfortably with the soles of your feet flat on the floor and preferably with your spine straight and your head slightly bowed. Allow your mind to reflect on your relationship. Consider your 'position' and name the negative feelings that resonated. Close your eyes and turn all your attention to your breathing. Consider inhaling and exhaling and work towards evenness in each breath. Slow your breathing down by taking slightly longer on each breath but maintain a rhythm that is entirely comfortable. Consider that breathing in and breathing out corresponds with action and receptivity. Create the reality of activity and stillness by breathing and resting. Assimilate the inhalation and exhalation with the acts of giving and receiving. Consider how healthy living is reflected in a balance of activity and stillness, giving and receiving.

2. Continue to remain aware of your breathing and now pay attention to your feet. Feel the soles of your feet flat on the floor and imagine growing roots out of your feet deep into the earth connecting you. Allow a very bright light from above to penetrate and surround every part of you. Now draw attention to the palms of your hands and imagine the light streaming from above, circulating through your body and pouring out of your palms. Continue to be mindful of your breathing, and remember the roots growing from the soles of your feet. In this stillness, reflections about you and your relationship may bring up painful emotions that you have not expressed in a long time. Allow yourself this process of feeling the feelings. If you feel resistance, just allow it. This is self-healing. Accept yourself fully, not for who or what you want to be but for who you really are right here and now. Know that over time you can change the things you don't like. By accepting yourself and acknowledging your suffering, you are giving yourself love and setting these emotions free.

3. Now feel your body. Are there any areas of tightness or heaviness? Are there any weak areas where you have endured injuries or illness? Are there any areas that need to be loved? Place your hands on these areas and give yourself healing to release any blockages and restore harmony. Do this for as long as is comfortable. When you are ready, give thanks for your ability to give care to yourself.

4. Now focus on any of the positive feelings that resonated and allow the feelings to spread to every part of your body. Immerse yourself in the feelings and allow this to energize you. Continue to breathe consciously. Draw more energy from the earth source through the roots and from the light source above you. Use your hands to channel the energy through your palms and once again place your hands any- where on your body that you are drawn to. When you are ready, give thanks for the stillness and the receiving and come back into everyday life, slowly and calmly.

Suggestions to Help with the Exercise

If you have never attempted an exercise like this you may find it hard to begin with. Like anything new, it takes time and practice. If the task seems daunting, start with smaller exercises over time to build up to the longer exercise; attend to your breathing a few times a day while going about your routine. On other occasions try imagining roots growing out of your feet while you are standing or sitting doing a boring task, such as the washing-up or the household accounts. Also try imagin- ing the beam of light coming down from above, surrounding you and penetrating you while you are in a queue at the shops. When those tasks become part of your routine, try putting them all together and doing the whole exercise.

This self-healing exercise is a building block to happiness in relationships. If you decide to skip it or even dismiss it as unnecessary you will need to go back and explore the section on resistance. It is very important to understand that should you choose not to give yourself any healing, acceptance and acknowledgement, your ability to give and receive in a relationship will be severely challenged.

PERCEPTION CHECKING

Once you are in the habit of self-healing and self-energizing you can move on from positions to perceptions. There is no such thing as one reality. There is only 'your' version of it, which is essentially your perception. What you believe to be true is only as true as your worldly experiences and what you tell yourself about those experiences.

You ADOPT A POSITION BASED on what you tell yourself, and this emerges from your perception of reality. You will find that you place greater value on experiences that reinforce your perceptions and reduce, dismiss or deny experiences that don't align with them. Perceptions that are left unchecked can lead to crises.

How a Situation Escalates

In this example of two of my clients, who we'll call Cindy and Max, it is very easy to see how situations escalate when there is an absence of dialogue:

Cindy had become close to a male colleague at work. She told Max, her husband, about John and how much she liked him. John and Cindy often went out together after work and Cindy seemed decidedly more alive. She began dressing differently and taking more care of her appearance. Max, fearing the worst, pretended not to care. If John's name was brought up, he would change the subject. Max found himself focusing some attention on a young girl at work who seemed to reciprocate. One thing led to another and Max ended up sleeping with her. In his mind he had settled a score because it was clear to him that Cindy was having an affair.

It all came out in a big argument, which resulted in Cindy walking out because she had not had an affair. In fact, John was gay and had been advising Cindy on clothes and make-up as she thought this would get Max's attention.

Max's perception had become his reality and he'd used this as a basis to act; however, the true reality was entirely different.

Achieving Success
Look again at the answers to the questions at the beginning of this chapter. Revisit your position and what it says about you. How much of it is what you are telling yourself and how much of it have you actually checked out with the other person in a collaborative conversation? Perception checking is vital for relationships to succeed. It enables us to accurately decode messages and avoid making assumptions.

Interpretations & Assumptions

Your partner has suddenly started checking emails and texts late at night and again first thing in the morning. Can you come up with three possible explanations for this sudden change in behaviour? Perhaps a surprise is being planned and your partner is awaiting some sort of confirmation? Maybe your partner is anxious about a sensitive piece of work that involves a number of participants? Or perhaps your partner has just bought a new phone and is now caught up in the technology? Put forward your own ideas.

Each one of those explanations is an interpretation or assumption. Without perception checking, the one I choose to be the 'truth' will determine what I say and do next. This is a recipe for conflict escalation because, if my perceptions are not true, my behaviour and actions will seem odd to my partner. This behaviour will be perceived by my partner in a certain way, and so on creating a vicious circle of miscommunication.

If my perceptions are not true, my behaviour and actions will seem odd to my partner.

OUR FUNDAMENTAL NEEDS

◆

The next piece of work in this chapter is to discover what is underneath all of this. Why exhaust ourselves with all this thinking and reflecting? Let's ask a different question. What is it that you want to achieve? Once you understand, you can begin to work towards it.

I F YOU ARE ANYTHING LIKE ME, you probably want to achieve peace of mind, love, trust, understanding, belonging, safety and togetherness in your relationships. These are our needs and they form the basis of what is important in life. Manfred Max-Neef, a Chilean economist, developed a table of fundamental human needs. He classifies these as:

- *Subsistence*
- *Understanding*
- *Creation*

- *Protection*
- *Participation*
- *Identity*

- *Affection*
- *Leisure*
- *Freedom*

The needs are defined through four categories: 'being, having, doing and interacting'. For example, the need for subsistence is met when you have physical and mental well-being. To have physical and mental well-being you need food, shelter and meaningful work. You can satisfy these needs by eating, clothing yourself, resting and working.

Max-Neef distinguishes our needs from satisfiers. Certain satisfiers, which are deemed to satisfy a particular need, in fact inhibit the possibility of satisfying other needs. For example, while watching television might be used to satisfy the need for recreation, it could limit creativity and participation. Do not confuse needs with satisfiers. Money is not a need; it is a satisfier that might satisfy the need for subsistence, freedom etc.

By considering the needs we are trying to meet and examining the satisfiers we are using to meet them, we can gain an in-depth insight into the problems we are trying to solve.

Now, take one need that is unmet in your relationship and explore it. Let's take intimacy as an example. If the need for intimacy is going unmet, what satisfiers are you using to achieve intimacy? And what satisfiers (like working long hours) are you using to meet other needs that inhibit intimacy?

Starting to Change

By now you will have some comprehension of what is going on in the relationship and how you are contributing to it. You are becoming aware; you are becoming mindful. So now ask yourself the following: What needs are not being fulfilled and what is the change I am seeking?

This is your starting point for change. Don't worry at this stage about whether you believe these changes are possible. If you have never examined yourself in this way and have struggled with it, take heart. I have been doing this for years and still struggle with owning my part in things, but familiarity with the process means that I can laugh at myself for being flawed and still enjoy and engage with the learning.

REFLECTIONS

If you have followed this chapter so far, you will have done some important groundwork. Ideally, you will both have done this piece of work separately but if only one of you has done it, you can still continue.

You will have solid outcomes for the following:

- Answers to some questions about the relationship in general.
- Ascertaining the current state of the relationship as you experience it.
- Working past blame and judgement.
- Owning and working on any resistances you might have.
- Working out your 'position' and what it might say about you.
- Identifying some words from the feelings spectrum to describe how you feel.
- Regular time-out sessions for self-healing and self-energizing.
- Reality testing your perceptions and what you tell yourself.
- Awareness of perceptions that have not been thoroughly checked out.
- Consciousness of what you are telling yourself.
- Knowing which of your needs are met or unmet.
- An understanding of the satisfiers you use to meet your needs.
- A clear starting point for the change you are seeking.

Give yourself some positive acknowledgement for getting to this stage. You can use the self-energizing technique and enjoy sitting with some positive feelings.

CHAPTER TWO

KNOWING YOURSELF

*You have just undertaken an individual
assessment of your relationship. The work you did
in the last chapter was focused on the dynamics of
the relationship you have with your partner and the
systems that you created to manage the relationship.
This chapter will focus on knowing yourself and
understanding how your relationship with
your partner affects you.*

SITTING WITH YOURSELF

◆

As this chapter is all about you, you are going to be asking yourself some rigorous questions and come face-to-face with yourself. You will develop emotional robustness through a process of compassionate honesty. The process of coming face-to-face with yourself has nothing to do with hard truths. Brutal honesty hurts and separates while compassionate honesty helps and connects.

WHEN WE PRACTISE COMPASSIONATE HONESTY, we first recognize that what we feel and need is important. We then learn how to ask for what we want in ways that are more likely to be heard and acted on by others. We learn how to deal with emotions that are blocking progress and we become able to respond in ways that are supportive and fulfilling. To do this, you will need to become more aware of your feelings and your needs, and the feelings and needs of others. To be in a healthy relationship you have to know yourself so that you can clearly understand your contribution to it and how what you do and what you say affects the dynamic.

If all this is new to you, it is probably because you have been used to suppressing your 'self'. When you suppress your self you deny your feelings and needs. A common response in someone suppressing their self is to answer with 'fine', when asked how they are. 'Fine' offers very little opportunity to connect yet it is a very common response. This tells me that

we have been conditioned by mainstream Western culture (which is fast becoming the global mainstream culture) to ignore our feelings and needs and submit to obedience and compliance for fear of standing out. When we submit to obedience we become punishable and replaceable.

Compliance does not create the conditions for emotional safety yet emotional safety is a really big need. In how many situations in your life do you actually tell the real truth? Do you modify what you really think or feel in order to be acceptable to your family, friends and colleagues? If you constantly find yourself modifying what you really think and feel, you will have little or no emotional support because you will have nowhere to air your true feelings.

◆

'Your task is not to seek for love, but merely to seek and find all the barriers within yourself that you have built against it.'

RUMI

◆

Communication

I remember working with a couple who wanted to improve their communication. We'll call them Rose and Richard. Rose needed emotional support, connection and affection, while Richard, the main provider of the family, seemed incapable of giving this. I asked him, 'How do you get emotional support?'

The question was incomprehensible to him; emotional support was just not on his radar. However, Richard gradually came to see how he had suppressed himself. In fact, he had carried such huge financial burdens on behalf of the family that he had almost forgotten that he existed as anything other than an achiever. He thought that anything less than providing increasing provision was a failure of his role in the eyes of Rose. His perception was that if he didn't fulfil the role he would be replaced and punished.

Richard therefore lied to himself and pretended that his feelings and needs didn't matter. He was really very frightened of the financial goals he was telling himself Rose had set for him, but which he had actually set for himself. To fulfil the role he had to switch off his true feelings. If he couldn't support his own emotions, then he certainly had no means of supporting his wife's. When I suggested that I would like to begin the sessions by doing some one-to-one work with Richard first, Rose was surprised.

As soon as Richard could understand the human need for emotional support and realize tangible benefits for himself from doing so, he found it easier to understand what Rose was looking for in their marriage.

LESSONS ABOUT LYING

◆

Lying can seem like a quick way out or a shortcut to something.
We do it when we feel some kind of pressure or tension in our lives.
However, lying breaches trust. When we lie to ourselves we stop
trusting ourselves. We do it because we are resisting change. Some-
where in ourselves we know that once the lid comes off, change will
be inevitable. So let's now take that lid off, and let's confront our-
selves with compassion and remain in charge of the process.

W E ALL LEARNED TO LIE FROM CHILDHOOD. We started
with little white lies and gradually built up to massive
whoppers. We saw our parents do it: you heard what your
parents said behind closed doors and this didn't match what
they told the neighbours. In turn, the neighbours told their
own lies. The people receiving the lies knew they were being
lied to and then they, in turn, lied back. It was an accepted
little circle of deception; it was a front to what was really
happening in their lives.

To some extent, we learned that pretending is the best way
to get through life. Since it is impossible to be good all of the
time, we exhaust a lot of energy in pretending to be good.
This manifests itself as manipulation, performing, withhold-
ing, exaggerating, concealing or using misleading information.
If we pretend for long enough, it becomes a way of life and it
embeds itself as part of our character or personality.

◆

'Your beliefs become your thoughts, your thoughts
become your words, your words become your actions,
your actions become your habits, your habits become
your values, your values become your destiny.'

MAHATMA GANDHI

◆

At its most prevalent we act out our lives instead of living our lives. When this happens we are lying to ourselves. We may even undergo personality tests, which categorize us by the strategies we use to get through life, and that's who we become. I know I have my work cut out when a client arrives and uses sentences that begin with, 'I'm the type of person who…', or 'People like me…'. This is not the real you. It is a construction that you thought would get you through life, but has actually imprisoned you.

Why Lie?

Lies are a natural form of emotional protection. Just as we would find immediate ways to protect ourselves from physical danger, so we also find ways to protect ourselves from emotional danger. If the truth is going to bring about punishment that will hurt, we will naturally take steps to protect ourselves from that hurt. And so we may lie.

An emotional punishment can be as simple as a parent withdrawing their love for their child for the next five minutes.

And it is worse when the punishment is not external. When there is no boss, no parent, no partner inflicting a punishment and you are doing it to yourself, it is considerably more difficult to run away and hide. It is your very own self-important internal police officer who criticizes and judges you, while you believe this is the self that you are answerable to.

Part of 'waking up' is realizing that the internal police officer is not you. It is a notional character who represents the mainstream society that you grew up in and who perpetuates all the beliefs you were told were truths. In our society there are authorities who expect you to obey and comply. If you don't obey then you have to find ways to pretend to be compliant or be punished. We have been taught to worry about what we are in the eyes of authority: 'How will I look?' or 'What will they say about me?' Much of our internal conversation is actually thrashed out in an imaginary courtroom where we are in the dock, being held accountable for ourselves.

Motivating Factors

The motivating factors behind our behaviour are often fear, guilt and shame. Think of how many tasks you have performed not because you wanted the opportunity to contribute, but because you were worried about the punishment or disapproval that was meted out if you didn't. So, you use your internal police officer to 'regulate' yourself. This is because what you think and feel and what you actually say and do are often poles apart. You think that if you let your feelings rule, your behaviour might become extreme; from either doing nothing or taking drastic action. You don't trust yourself enough, so you continue to defer to the internal police officer.

Can you see how all this makes the fundamental basis of your inner regulation dishonest and unsustainable? We learned this form of regulation from people in the past who could not predict the way of life we would have today. The rate of change has exceeded what most people could have dreamed of, and the tools we were handed will not do the job. In fact, the tools are a source of stress.

QUALITY OF LIFE

To fully engage in any relationship, you first have to have a sound and fulfilling relationship with yourself and relieve yourself of stress. You need to take responsibility for the quality of your life on a continuous and conscious basis. To do this, you have to let go of the old ways of doing things and introduce a new way of being. The new way of being could be defined as mindfulness.

MINDFULNESS IS ABOUT BEING IN THE PRESENT without commenting or judging; just noticing. If I decide to become aware of my left foot, I come into the present. I am now noticing my foot and any sensations in it; it is warm in

my slipper right now. I don't judge that; I simply notice it. Now, as I sit and type in front of my computer screen and keyboard I notice that my back is not comfortable in the chair. It hurts slightly so I ask myself if I want to do anything about it. Now a conflict arises in me. One part of me wants to move and find some other cushions to try and another part of me wants to complete this section before moving.

This is about knowing myself and being able to sit with my feelings. I choose not to react but to reflect on the whole circumstance before taking any action. I feel a slight irritation with myself. I don't know which of my needs to put first; my need for physical comfort or my need for completion?

Before I knew my 'self', this was a type of dilemma that I would never have noticed. In suppressing my 'self' I programmed myself to keep going; get the job done at all costs. Of course, then I would be tired and irritable when I really wanted to be playful and alive with my children as they were growing up. Another issue was that as I began to consider my 'self' I became disproportionately aware of every discomfort and of wanting to ensure my needs were met as a priority. Now the pendulum has swung both ways and settled in the middle place, and I can accept that I am conflicted in myself, but that I am also OK.

By being honest, considering my feelings in the moment and being OK with what I am sensing, I have made the point, finished the section and resolved the situation for myself.

CREATING AN INTERNAL GARDEN

◆

Knowing yourself is all about sending the internal police officer off on indefinite leave. If he (or she) pops back from time to time, just remind him that he is on leave and send him on his way. Now, with all that lovely internal space we can create a garden, a place of cultivation, growth, beauty, relaxation and play.

TAKE SOME TIME TO THINK about how you would like your garden to be. Remember, it is your garden and it will be a reflection of you. The theme is contentment. Let your imagination run free to include anything that will help you to feel content. Spend some time creating your garden; you might want to draw it or write about it or find images that represent it. One useful way is to make a collage, but only if you would enjoy doing that.

Whatever way you choose to bring the garden to life, this exercise requires you to spend a bit of time reflecting, imagining, creating and reviewing. When you have completed it, ask yourself what the garden provides for you. You may also want to refer back to the needs section in Chapter One. Here are some more needs that may resonate with you:

Remember, it is your garden and it will be a reflection of you.

SOCIAL NEEDS

Acceptance
Acknowledgement
Affection
Affirmation
Appreciation
Autonomy
Belonging
Celebration
Choice
Closeness
Collaboration
Communication
Companionship
Compassion
Completion
Consideration

Consistency
Contact
Contribution
Cooperation
Ease
Empathy
Equality
Help
Honesty
Humour
Inclusion
Intimacy
Joy
Mourning
Mutuality
Nurturing

Participation
Planning
Presence
Reassurance
Recognition
Respect
Security
Sharing
Solidarity
Stability
Structure
Support
Tolerance
Trust
Understanding
Warmth

SPIRITUAL NEEDS

Adventure
Authenticity
Balance
Beauty
Challenge
Clarity
Competence
Creativity
Discovery
Effectiveness
Freedom
Freshness

Fun
Growth
Harmony
Hope
Imagination
Independence
Inspiration
Integrity
Learning
Love
Meaning
Mystery

Order
Peace
Play
Power
Purpose
Rhythm
Self-expression
Space
Spontaneity
Stimulation
Variety
Wholeness

PHYSICAL NEEDS

Air
Food
Light
Movement

Nourishment
Protection
Rest
Safety

Sexual expression
Shelter
Touch
Warmth

Finding Contentment

Now imagine placing a bridge from your day-to-day life into your garden. Whenever you feel stressed you can close your eyes, walk across the bridge and step into the garden. As you walk across the bridge, you will have your back towards your day-to-day life and you will be facing and entering the beauty of your garden of contentment.

You are going to begin practising what it feels like to be content. You are going to see how long you sit in that place before the messengers of the day come and get you. This is a really important piece of learning. How long can you stay in the place of contentment? We will go into this in more depth when we get back to thinking about the relationship.

Going to your garden is taking a break. Imagine you are walking around all day every day carrying two heavy suitcases. One is called the past and contains all the guilt, shame and resentment about what has happened in your life. The other is called the future and contains all the worries, anxieties and fears about what might happen going forward. No matter how much you want to get to your destination, you know it makes sense to take regular breaks and put the suitcases down. Resting gives you strength, refreshes you and helps you find new perspectives. Going into your garden does the same. We place importance on our physical health; eating healthily, exercising etc., which is of course needed, but we need to place equal importance on our emotional health, too.

GUIDED VISIONING

We are beginning the process of visioning. Guided visioning is a popular way of defining and achieving a desirable outcome because if we can see it, and imagine the steps that are needed to get there, we are more likely to achieve it. The practice of visioning will help you to achieve a state of relaxed awareness. This is all about being in the present moment and going about your normal activities with a confident and relaxed approach.

U SING GUIDED VISIONING helps you notice what is going on around you but you don't submit to fight or flight impulses. Instead, you are aware of your circumstances and in any unexpected situation you can adapt and strategize according to what is needed moment by moment. Guided visioning engages us in conceptual thinking. It is a magical mystery tour in your own mind where you expand beyond the norms of your day-to-day and discover more of what you have inside you.

Self-knowing & Self-understanding

Make some time to compare your day-to-day life with your life in your garden. Describe the feelings that most pervade your everyday life. You might want to go back to the feelings lists in Chapter One (see pages 23–24). Take some time to sense those feelings and notice how they affect your body. Look for any tightness or tension. Now repeat the exercise,

naming the feelings that you most feel in your relationship. And repeat the exercise again, naming the feelings that come up when you are in your garden of contentment.

These are your feelings. They reflect how you are in different situations: day-to-day, in your relationship and in your garden. Ask yourself: 'What is different about these situations?', 'What is similar about these situations?', 'What is it about these situations that generates such feelings?'

If you find yourself judging and blaming others for how you feel, stop. How you feel is no one else's responsibility. How you feel is what you generate in response to incidents and circumstances. One phrase I would love to delete from our language is, 'How does that make you feel?' No one can 'make' you feel anything. The only question is, 'How do you feel when…' followed by a description of the incident or action, for example: 'How do you feel when…' '…I say I love you', or '…you remember our argument?' or '…I am late'.

Feelings can only be processed in the present. How you felt last week or last year is not what we are processing. We are connecting with how you feel right now when you imagine or remember something that happened.

If you find yourself judging and blaming others for how you feel, stop.

GETTING ACQUAINTED WITH FEELINGS

◆

Our feelings are a natural alarm system that lets us know that we have some emotional work to do. For that alarm system to work, we need to have a vocabulary of feelings. While we can recognize feelings when they are described, the intensity and range of feelings that arise are a unique combination in each of us.

I LEARNED FROM MY GREATEST TEACHER, Dr Marshall Rosenberg, that feelings are due to a particular need in a person being met or unmet. And herein lies the importance of feelings and the reason why we should spend time getting acquainted with the whole spectrum. Why would you want to spend any time dwelling on negative feelings? Surely it is better to push them away and think positive? It depends on how you view negative feelings. What if negative feelings are a doorway into learning and self-development? Then surely you will look forward to engaging with them? Does this sound impossible to you? It really is just practice. The more you engage with feelings the less disturbing they become. The more you learn about who you are and what you project out in the world, the more you will understand and the more confident you will become.

In fact, it is really helpful to learn to name the feelings and notice them as they are happening. If those feelings are there and you suppress them they will leak out of you in other ways, through your body and through your relationships. The more you attempt to suppress them the bigger they will become and the more fear you will build in facing up to them.

Now take a feeling and relate it to an unmet need. Look at the needs list earlier in the chapter and find out which unmet need is triggering the feeling.

Feeling Reluctance

Let's say a situation has arisen in which I am asked to do something I don't want to do. There are reasons for this but I am weighing up the costs of doing it or not. The reluctance stems from my need to be understood, but I don't trust the other person has the time or capacity to understand how much I have on my plate. So I have to give understanding to myself.

I understand that I have an inner conflict and that I want to solve the dilemma and I understand my own discomfort. I also know that it is no one else's fault that I have a lot going on. I don't want anyone to see me as unapproachable and feel unable to make a request of me. I have enough self-knowledge to choose which requests I agree to with a good heart and the confidence to choose which requests I refuse in a way that doesn't leave the other person believing they were wrong for asking.

Now I will weigh up what needs of mine would be met and unmet if I followed my immediate impulse and refused to do the task. If I don't do the task, my need for participation, sharing and wholeness will go unmet, while the only needs

that will be met are my needs for structure and autonomy (and as I grow older I am not placing such a high value on these particular needs).

When you piece a problem like this together by examining needs you will probably come up with a different answer. Every answer is acceptable. Spend some time examining your needs. Consider those needs that consistently go unmet in your life and work out what it is you do to keep it that way. Here are some key points to consider about needs:

• Needs are not the same as satisfiers so concentrate on ensuring that you are not replacing needs with satisfiers. An item or an action is not a need but a satisfier, which might meet the need.

• All actions are attempts to meet needs, which can fail spectacularly. I am unlikely to meet my need for respect if I am shouting angrily at someone, yet my need for respect is universal in my life.

• I don't only have needs for myself; I would also like to see those needs met in others because this feels great for everyone.

• The optimum position is to meet needs equally; not for one person to meet their own needs at a cost to another's.

• It is my responsibility to get my needs met but meeting my needs may best be assisted by making requests of others.

• The joy of life is the state of contentment that arises from accepting that in any one moment not all your needs will be met but, in a free society, you can choose what you do about it.

Now look at what needs of your own are met and unmet in your day-to-day life, in your relationship and in your garden of contentment and consider the following questions:

• What specific needs are consistently being met or unmet throughout your life?

• What needs are met or unmet in particular situations? If you find any needs unmet in your garden, make any additions or adjustments you like to get the garden to meet your needs.

• What do you do to meet your needs?

• What thoughts, behaviours or actions do you engage in that do not meet your needs?

The last question in this list is where you really come face-to-face with yourself. Answering this question with complete honesty will become the starting point for self-responsibility and empowerment.

Self-acceptance

In my own life I recognize there are a few things that I do that definitely do not meet my needs. One example is displaying impatience in my tone and manner. I do this because I want to be heard and understood, yet I am aware that displaying impatience is the least likely way to engage another person to hear and understand me.

When I really came to this awareness, I used it as a starting point for learning a better way of communicating. I am now a mediator. To be a mediator I have to slow down, listen, hear

and understand the people who come to mediation and be a living demonstration of how to do that. I learned the skills and developed them. Now I can get myself heard and understood in most situations. I still lapse into impatience from time to time and I realize that when I demonstrate impatience, the consequence of not being heard and understood is mostly attributable to my inability to articulate in a way that engages the other person.

Finding this place within yourself is a crucial first step in participating in a healthy relationship. Allowing yourself to be in touch with your own limiting behaviour is very liberating because it gives you freedom to choose what aspects you want to change and what you want to keep.

Now accept yourself for who you really are and celebrate. Take time out to be you; sit with yourself in the knowledge of all that you are. Include all the bits you really like and all the rubbish bits that make you a wonderfully flawed and imperfect human being. Let imperfect be perfect.

Go back to the self-healing and self-energizing exercise and re-read it. Sit comfortably and begin with the breathing. Close your eyes and grow roots from the soles of your feet. Connect with the beam of light from above and now slowly cross the bridge into your garden of contentment. Imagine yourself sitting in the garden or lying on the grass and breathe in all its beauty, contentment and love. Breathe out love, gratitude and growth.

TIME TO FORGIVE

◆

The best definition of forgiveness I have ever heard is: 'Forgiveness is letting go of all hope for a better past.' In this context, forgiveness becomes vital to living in the present. In one of your self-healing and self-energizing sessions, heal the past with forgiveness: forgiveness of those around you and forgiveness of yourself.

B EGIN THIS SESSION with your forgiveness of others; this is usually quite easy. Just remember and forgive. Remain mindful of our definition of forgiveness. Forgiving others does not mean that you should accept behaviours or actions that affect you in the present. It simply means you cannot change what has gone before and you allow a new starting point for change.

Forgiveness is letting go of all hope for a better past.

Now forgive yourself. Forgiving yourself is often more difficult than forgiving others because we are usually much harder on ourselves. When I did this exercise during my Reiki Level 2 initiation, I was moved to tears. It was a mixture of both giving myself permission and then experiencing the sheer relief of letting go. So, when you do this exercise make sure you have given yourself enough time and space to fully feel and be with yourself. A box of tissues might come in handy, too.

A Note About Resentment

I met an Iraqi woman while on introductory training. Though her English wasn't good and we occasionally had difficulty communicating, I learned that she had been imprisoned and tortured in Iraq during Saddam Hussein's regime and had to flee the country. Her father and brothers had been killed. She had only one fundamental question: What drives one human being to be violent to another? She carried no hatred towards those who had hurt her, only questions.

I was very moved by her courage and compassion so I invited her to be part of some high-level mediation training, designed to train a group of people to mediate violent conflicts. She came along to the training sessions and found some answers to her questions; namely that a person resorts to violence when they are not heard in the way they want to be heard, when they can't express themselves in a way that gets them understood and when they simply can't understand the other person.

With this knowledge she went on to develop her own training course and she mediates violent family conflicts. She represents someone who has truly suffered, rid herself of the burden of resentment and transformed her life on the principles of non-violence. Her commitment to compassionate honesty is an inspiration to me.

Free Yourself

If you are experiencing difficulty with the idea of forgiving, ask yourself these questions in relation to whatever you have been through: How did it help me to be stronger? If you have come out the other side of a tough time then something in you will be stronger. What do I know now that I didn't know before? Likewise, tough times give us new insight or open up new questions. Has this experience in some way met my need for learning and growth even though it was a painful way to learn? Am I tangled up in shame? When shame manifests itself as a feeling that you're damaged and fundamentally different from other people, go back to your feelings and needs. You can transcend this shame by naming some other feelings and needs. Finally, am I feeling resentment? When resentment surfaces it is useful to learn from Nelson Mandela's famous quote: 'Resentment is like drinking poison and waiting for it to kill your enemy.' Free yourself.

Resentment is like drinking poison and waiting for it to kill your enemy.

REFLECTIONS

In working through this chapter you will have:

- Understood the importance of releasing yourself from suppression.
- Uncovered any lies you have been telling yourself.
- Signed off from your internal police officer.
- Discovered your true feelings and needs.
- Created a garden of contentment.
- Become honest with yourself about the things you do that do not meet your needs.

Now reflect on these positioning statements:

- Acceptance of yourself and everything that makes you the person you are.
- Clarity on who you are and what you do.
- Understanding of where you are in your life and how you contributed to it.
- Curiosity as to how your life can be different and better.

CHAPTER THREE

RECEIVING
YOUR PARTNER

*In the last chapter we were concentrating
on you; now we move on to concentrate on your
partner. Your partner's behaviour stems from
whatever is not working within your relationship.
External factors such as work or extended family
problems may cloud the issues, but just as you
have worked on understanding your own sources
of unhappiness, now you will find out what
affects your partner's happiness.*

BECOMING A LISTENER

◆

If you are working through this book alone, you are taking on the task of leading the change in your relationship. If you are working through this book together you will both have completed the previous stages. Note that until now, the exercises have been conducted separately and you have not been invited to exchange ideas or consult with your partner. In this chapter you will be finding out about your partner.

TO RECEIVE YOUR PARTNER YOU WILL NEED SOME SKILLS:

• **LISTENING** Giving your partner enough space to fully express themselves; feeding back accurately what you hear and asking encouraging questions.

• **RAPPORT BUILDING** Creating the sense that your partner's feelings and needs are understood; giving them a chance to work at their own pace and demonstrating a believable interest in helping your communication.

• **FACILITATION** Helping your partner to express their emotions and concerns.

• **CONFLICT MANAGEMENT** Remaining calm and encouraging communication even when you hear something you don't like. Responding to strong feelings with empathy.

The skills are linked to a set of qualities, which are listed opposite. By learning the skills, the qualities develop and grow and the skills then become easier to practise.

• **UNDERSTANDING OF SITUATIONS & PEOPLE** Being aware of various different kinds of behaviour and taking a compassionate view of the reasons for those behaviours.

• **ABILITY TO LEARN FROM EXPERIENCE** Developing a willingness to build on your current knowledge and understanding of self and others.

• **GENUINENESS** Compassionate understanding of your own strengths and weaknesses, combined with a willingness to show vulnerability.

• **OPENNESS TO OTHER PEOPLE** Respecting differences with an awareness of your own triggers.

• **SELF-AWARENESS** Being aware of your feelings and needs and not imposing them onto others.

• **FLEXIBILITY** Being able to change and adapt according to the needs of the moment.

• **ANALYTICAL ABILITY** Realistically assessing chances of change; knowing when to continue and when to stop.

'When you meet someone better than yourself,

turn your thoughts to becoming his equal.

When you meet someone not as good as you are,

look within and examine yourself.'

CONFUCIUS

A Note About Engagement

In the area of the community where I have been working, I came across a rather formidable man, both in his physical size and character. Local people have strong opinions about him. When I first met him he would talk in a way that seemed angry and intimidating to me. However, he has access to and influences hundreds, if not thousands of young people so it occurred to me that what he had to say could be important and the messages he could pass on might also be significant.

I listened through the surface anger and heard some very important content about the needs of young people. I was very keen to hear more but he was suspicious of my motives and did not trust me. Of couse, he had no reason to trust me because I had not earned any trust. After about a year of consistent attempts at engagement, an opportunity arose and he agreed to talk to me.

The last three years of collaboration have been a privilege. He attended the high-level mediation training I ran and while I taught him some skills, he taught me how to open my eyes to marginalized and disempowered youth. Despite the differences in our backgrounds and outlook, this unlikely partnership has resulted in some very powerful community engagement projects and a lasting and enduring friendship.

PREPARING TO ENGAGE WITH A PARTNER

◆

First ask yourself if you are in good enough shape to hear and receive your partner. Being in good enough shape means feeling rested and resourced enough to hear things you might not like and being clear about your ability to remain calm and non-reactive. If the answer is no or if you find yourself judging and blaming, do not brush it aside but continue by following the steps outlined below.

Go BACK AND EXPLORE YOURSELF. Give yourself self-healing and self-energizing as described in Chapter One. Revisit the forgiveness exercise. It might be that you have been operating so far out of your tolerances for so long that it is hard to find a path back to being OK.

If you are doing this process alone and you are leading the change and you still hold resentment or hostility towards your partner in your heart, I would strongly urge you to consider whether you are in a place to do 'leadership' right now. It may be better to go and ask your partner if they will embark on this process with you. Or you might want to talk to a counsellor or friend who has the appropriate skills to support you through this.

If you haven't been able to accept yourself and open your heart to what is coming next, the buck stops with you and you will need assistance before proceeding to the next stage. Finding help is a gift and a wonderful way of looking after

yourself. If you are still resisting, ask yourself how else you might achieve what it is you wanted when you decided to read this book, and change course if necessary.

Preparing for Engagement

Let's assume that you have come this far and you are ready to continue. The next step is to get engagement. Whether you want this relationship to stay together or to break up, gaining and retaining engagement is the best way forward if you want the least amount of suffering for everyone involved. One of my friends, Paul Baker, runs a company that has been working to develop a framework for people to work together and create the best conditions for all, even in difficult and challenging situations. He calls it a 'systemic win' as opposed to a 'win/win' situation. He puts it very well: 'If you don't care what happens to the person you are in conflict with or if you want them hurt, damaged or destroyed, can they intelligently do anything except defend themselves against you even if it perpetuates the conflict?' I admire this perspective.

CREATING THE CONDITIONS
FOR ENGAGEMENT

◆

The first and most important part of approaching engagement is to create the conditions in which your partner feels emotionally safe to engage. You will need to demonstrate that you can be trusted and that things are going to change. You will also need to ask permission to engage and arrange a time to talk.

I F UP UNTIL NOW YOU HAVE BEEN LIBERAL with your voicing of judgements and labels – to put it bluntly – if you have regularly called your partner 'lazy' and 'good-for-nothing', 'loud-mouthed' and 'controlling', or if you have chosen silence and passivity as your means of protection, you are going to have to demonstrate that you are changing and doing things differently. Trust will not come easily or quickly. Dr Marshall Rosenberg has written a number of songs that illustrate learning points and he sings them in his workshops. This verse from 'Song from Brett' makes the point:

> *'Now even if you change your style*
> *It will take me a little while*
> *Before I can forgive and forget*
> *Because it seemed to me that you*
> *Couldn't see me as human too*
> *Until all your standards were met.'*

Asking Permission to Engage

It is important to check out and respect another person's capacity to engage. So, the first task is to ask if it is OK to talk. The only outcome you are looking for at this stage is an agreement to engage. It doesn't have to be now, in fact it is better if you get an agreement and then set a time so your partner can prepare. And it helps to choose your moment. I wouldn't expect a positive result if I began this dialogue five minutes before my partner is due to leave for an important meeting or in the middle of his favourite television show. With that in mind, here is a suggested approach: 'Is it OK for me to talk to you right now for about two to three minutes?', or 'Is it OK if I interrupt you right now for a couple of minutes?'

This question is a small opening step. It tests the water for engagement. It makes a very clear request for a short amount of time. If the answer is no, I would next ask when a good time might be and then try again at that time. Since this is your partner and you have mutual interests, it would be very unusual for the person to refuse entirely to ever talk to you.

Remember that tone, body language and choice of words are really important. When a person has become defensive, they are listening acutely for anything that justifies their defensiveness so any slight inflection may set off a trigger in them. And remember you are only doing this exercise when your own triggers are under control and you have given yourself care and understanding.

There are some important things to learn about making requests of others:

• If you know you will feel angry or upset by someone's refusal to meet your request then you are not making a request, you are making a demand.

• If your intention is to get your own way, you are making a demand.

• When you make demands, you are taking away the other person's freedom to choose.

• If you take away a person's freedom to choose, they are likely to retaliate in order to try to meet their needs for freedom and choice.

• If a person agrees to a request out of anything other than a voluntary willingness to contribute, you are not achieving healthy communication.

• If your intention is to understand whatever is getting in the way of your request and be open to finding another way of asking, then you are making a request.

• A true request is an invitation to contribute to your well-being and your life together, to which the other person is free to say 'no'. Instead of asking: 'Could you not leave your clothes on the chair?' try asking: 'Would you help me by putting your clothes away?' Saying: 'You never put your clothes away,' has no request in it at all and is an unhelpful attempt at an observation. Notice how all three versions of this question give off a completely different energy.

Arranging a Time to Talk

At the point where you have engagement for two to three minutes, you need to state your business and make a simple, clear, do-able request. For example, I might say, 'I really want to understand our relationship better and to do that I need to understand you better. I would like to arrange a time for us to sit down together where I can really learn about how you are because I realize that I have been absorbed in other things for quite a while. Would you be willing to set aside some time for us to do that?'

At that point I would hope to get out diaries and make a date. If you get objections and resistance, don't be tempted to enter the arena. Be clear that you really only wanted to take up two or three minutes right now to arrange a time to talk. Explain how important it is that you and your partner both feel relaxed and prepared to have a quality conversation together. Stay calm and reassure your partner that you are not avoiding any questions or comments. You want to be sure that you have set aside the time to fully understand the situation but you are not ready right now as you hadn't expected so much interaction about it.

If you have a day and time set, thank your partner for helping and for getting on board. And thank yourself. You have come a long way to get this far and you will have already learned a lot about the relationship. Now you will be entering the domain of collaboration and dialogue.

Refusal to Engage

In the unlikely circumstance that you are faced with a total refusal to engage, I would ask if the person could ever imagine a time when they would feel able to talk, or how they imagine the issues might be resolved without communication. I would also consider using a mediator. When my second marriage ended, we used mediation to discuss the outstanding issues. Like most breakups, it was difficult and painful, but the fact that we were both willing to work through a mediator did make a huge difference to the ending. But this book is not for those extreme circumstances where all communication has broken down; its aim is to help make the existing communication better, so let's get back to the initial request.

Growing the Relationship Together

By now I hope that you are realizing that a relationship is something that is created, planned, built, reviewed and refined. It doesn't just happen without any thought or consideration. There is a general view about relationships that they begin with an initial passion, which wears off, and then the relationship settles into companionship or complacency, and there are plenty of examples all around us that reinforce this very limiting belief.

But what if you didn't have to settle for companionship and complacency? What if it were completely possible to find a partner and grow together combining intimacy, trust and understanding with adventure, challenge and self-expression? Well, it is if you are prepared to invest some energy into making it so, and if you are willing to confront conflict with compassion. What you are about to do is part of the process.

Back to the Garden

Go back to your garden of contentment. Cross the bridge, admire your garden and find a comfortable place to sit. Connect to your breathing. As you sit in your garden, imagine that at the end of your garden there is another garden backing onto yours. This is your partner's garden. Can you see into the garden? Is there a wall or hedge or some other boundary between the gardens that blocks the view? Is it easy to access? What does the garden look like? How does that garden affect you? Can you still sit in your garden of contentment peacefully?

Take time to wander around, noticing any feelings and sensations in your body. When you're ready, imagine you are about to cross into your partner's garden. Consider the UK Country Code: 'Bring nothing but wonder, leave nothing but footprints, take nothing but photographs.'

Imagine that at the end of your garden there is another garden backing onto yours. This is your partner's garden.

PREPARING FOR DIALOGUE

◆

Remember this isn't about you. You are preparing for a tour of your partner's thoughts and feelings. You will need to put all your own triggers and opinions to one side. You are not there as a judge or defender of anything. You are a clear channel ready to receive whatever is presented in the moment, so before you start ensure that you are not rushed or pressured by any distractions.

MAKE SURE YOU ARE SITTING in a way that allows you to have eye contact. If you are tactile as a couple you might want to sit holding hands, turned towards each other.

Allow 20 minutes before the start time to self-energize. Consider what you are about to do and what you hope the outcomes will be. Create a private and comfortable space both environmentally and energetically. Connect with your breathing, take a few minutes to give yourself some understanding and come into the present moment. Temporarily suspend everything around you and let go in the now.

As we go through the dialogue, I will offer up the words that I would use. It is important that you use language that is natural to you. As you adapt my script, take care to be mindful of what you say:

- *Check the intention*
- *Check for any trigger words*
- *Check your tone and manner*

How to Respond to Your Partner

When you begin a dialogue, you should always allow your partner to finish what they are saying before you respond. Even if you don't like what you hear, resist the temptation to interrupt. Hearing something you don't like is part of learning.

If your partner is not working through this book with you and you are leading this process, it is likely that your partner will use language of blame and judgement. Whatever happens, do not correct what is said. In a relationship, it is important that we create the conditions where we can tell each other our most private thoughts and feel sure that the contents will not be used as ammunition either now or at a later date.

Undertaking the Exercise

When you are both feeling comfortable, begin with a simple introduction. 'Thanks for agreeing to do this. My intention is to hear fully what you have to say and to do that, I want to ask you some questions. The questions are just here to help me begin, so please say whatever is in your heart. The only thing I want from you right now is some trust and a willingness to engage. Once you've answered the question I am going to tell you what I heard you say so that you can check whether I am on the same page as you.'

The purpose of this exercise is to hear your partner in the way they want to be heard. Before you start the exercise it is worth remembering that in recent times it has become far

easier to jump ship from an unhappy relationship and, while there can be many good reasons to do so, good communication skills remain important for a healthy relationship.

This is especially important if you are breaking up a relationship where children are involved. If you are struggling with communication in this relationship you may well find the same issues cropping up in your next one. Like anything else in life, it only ends when you decide to give up. One of my favourite quotes of unknown origin is: 'Everything will be alright in the end. If it's not alright it's just not the end yet.'

QUESTIONS TO WORK THROUGH

In this section you will be given some questions to work through. Notice how the questions are designed to encourage descriptive answers and not just generate yes or no replies. Read through the questions that have been suggested along with the guidance provided and decide which ones are relevant to your relationship.

As you ask each relevant question, as listed below, your partner will give you an answer. If you get monosyllabic answers, ask for some elaboration: 'It would really help me if you could say a bit more because I want to be sure I am clear about your thoughts and feelings and it's difficult when I have so little to go on.' Wait until your partner has finished speaking and then respond by telling them what you heard them say. Remember you can never tell another person what they said, only what you heard.

- *What do you think about our relationship?*
- *What is a relationship to you?*
- *How do you see your role in this relationship?*
- *How do you see my role in this relationship?*
- *What do we do well as a couple?*
- *What could we individually improve on?*
- *How does the future of our relationship look?*

Do not be tempted to ask any further questions or to stray into opinion sharing.

When you tell your partner what you heard they will probably want to adjust or amend their account slightly. Allow this to happen because it is not very often that we get to hear a reflection of our own words. Usually when we speak, the person listening replies with an opinion or counter argument and the conversation builds on agreement or disagreement. Here, we are not out to prove a point or find a conclusion; we are making space for exploration and discovery through dialogue. If your partner adjusts their answer, simply let them know you have heard that adjustment by once again repeating back what you have heard.

In the training sessions I run, the participants often find this tricky. It takes time to get used to this process. Try not to substitute your own words or summarize.

Listening & Repeating

Let's say your partner responds to the question, 'What do we do well as a couple?' with: 'I don't know; we fight a lot and it's been a long time since we did anything nice together.' If you are repeating what you heard, it might sound something like: 'Because we fight a lot and because it's been a long time since we did anything nice together, you don't know what it is that we do well together?'

But if you repeat back with: 'So you think we don't do anything well together?', you have made an interpretation of their response and presented something different. If you do this, you will find it difficult to build trust and rapport with your partner because they will worry that you are not fully hearing them. They will let you know by continually adjusting and amending their response and finally, perhaps, running out of patience. If this happens, don't give up. If this is the first time you have attempted anything like this, take heart. You have done amazingly well to get this far.

If your relationship is really suffering, then think about how long it took to get to the point where you felt unhappy. You probably weren't unhappy at the beginning; it took some time for happiness to transform into unhappiness. Likewise, it will take time to get back to happiness. If you have painted yourself into a communications corner, it will take time to figure out how to get out of it without making a mess and it might take several attempts.

At this point, you have been through the questions, heard your partner's responses and restated their ideas and feelings to their satisfaction. Now ask you partner if they trust that you have heard them correctly. If the answer is yes, you can move on to the next step. If you get a response other than yes, continue to work on this phase.

Check out whether there is anything that might have been missed or that should be taken into account and once again, repeat back what you heard. Once you have moved on from the listening and repeating stage, check that your partner has finished giving their account.

Show You Have Understood

Now let your partner know that you have understood their responses. First, tell them that the questions are over. Thank them for cooperating and then ask permission to state your understanding. I might say something like: 'Thank you for telling me all this; it's been very helpful. Now I'd like to tell you what I have understood from everything you said so you know what I will be reflecting on. Is that OK?'

Displaying Empathy

You will now be empathizing with your partner's position. To do this, we should define empathy for the purposes of this exercise. Empathy is the ability to recognize and understand the feelings of another person. Empathy is a state without

words so we use words to show that we are in empathy. When we have empathy we allow the other person the full extent of their own feelings without solving, criticizing, judging or competing with our own story.

How many times did you tell someone about an incident only to have to listen to a comparable incident? Was it satisfying? No, because you were robbed of your own conflict. How many times did you tell someone about your feelings only for them to offer a strategy that instructed you to take an action: 'Tell him to get lost,' or attempted to change your feelings: 'Never mind. Cheer up'?

In empathy, we are truly allowing the other person to have their feelings and for those feelings to be OK. I usually address the situation by naming the feelings and working to find out what needs are unmet. If someone wants to tell me about something that has happened, I will usually ask outright whether they simply want me to listen or whether they want my advice. Their answer will help me to settle into what is expected of me and therefore make me a better listener.

If you have not done any self-development work with yourself, you will find it difficult to do with another person. This is where you should notice that you're reaping all the benefits of the work you did with yourself in Chapter Two.

To conclude this tour, you are going to summarize your understanding of your partner's account by relating it to a set of feelings and needs. Of course, nothing is more annoying than telling someone how they feel. You can only ever guess and, often, it isn't helpful just to describe someone as angry. If you have listened, you will be able to guess the needs behind all the statements. You may find it helpful to return to the lists of feelings and needs in Chapters One and Two (see pages 23–24, 31 and 45).

Closing the Session

Here's an example of how a situation might be summarized. You might say: 'If I understand you correctly, you are worried about the state of our relationship. You want me to be less impatient when things go wrong and you want us to be closer. I'm guessing that you feel some frustration when I get stressed with you because you're really needing my understanding.'

You may or may not have guessed correctly; it doesn't matter. The whole point is to demonstrate you care by trying. Your partner will let you know the answer and you can explore the lists together to really identify feelings and needs.

If this has gone according to plan, then you have truly received your partner. You need to close this session so that you both understand what will happen next. Often, when you get to this point the other person might begin to ask about how you are. For now, I want you to thank them for asking and say that you don't want to change the focus from them. Explain that you have heard some really useful comments and you want to reflect on them before proceeding.

If you got this far and your partner participated in the exercise but you didn't enjoy their responses, this is a signal for you to develop your listening skills. It might be that your tolerance for listening is lower than you imagined or you find it difficult to hear without judging. Whatever the reason, this is your present state and your starting point for learning. The point of being mindful is to accept where you are right here and now; notice it, allow it and accept it.

REFLECTIONS

Before moving on you can review your learning so far by:

- Assessing your skills and qualities.
- Making a plan to develop your skills.
- Checking how you reacted if you experienced any resistance from your partner.
- Checking how you responded if you heard any things you didn't like.
- Describing your partner's feelings and needs in the context of the relationship.
- Describing what you know now that you didn't know before.

If you have a sense of progress then you might like to mark this with your partner with something you would consider to be a treat. That could be an exchange of gifts, a card or a dinner.

CHAPTER FOUR

THE TASK AHEAD

So far the journey has been researching, exploring and positioning your relationship. Now you should pause and allow all that has taken place in your life to be fully part of your current situation. This is a place of consideration and acceptance. Everything in the past becomes present — without excusing it, exaggerating it, minimizing it or dismissing it. Here you begin to imagine and create your own future. You will realize the issues and be mindful. This is the place where you turn a corner.

ALLOWING THE PROCESS

◆

Up until now you have been preparing the foundations for change. It is time to ponder on the information you have gathered and begin working out the real issues. This requires a period of reflection and consideration for you and your partner. You should have a wealth of raw material to begin to process and mould. Now place the raw materials into your subconscious and ask it to digest the information. You will come back to it in a few days.

THE REST OF THIS CHAPTER contains a series of ideas and propositions. There is no work to do except to read and notice what resonates. This is your 'now' and you need to give it your full attention because the past and the future do not materially exist; they are notions based on your perceptions and positions. All the people involved in your life will have different notions of the past and the present even though you journeyed through the same events in the past and plan to be at the same events in the future. We spend so much time living in the future, imagining what it will be like when a task is done, when we have achieved this goal or acquired that item and we do this at the expense of living life fully in the present. We are impatient and don't want to sit with the uncertainty because the 'not knowing' triggers discomfort in us. We distract from discomfort in all sorts of ways, such as starting an argument or shopping for something we don't need.

'Have patience with everything that remains unsolved in your heart. Try to love the questions themselves, like locked rooms and like books written in a foreign language. Do not now look for the answers. They cannot now be given to you because you could not live them. It is a question of experiencing everything. At present you need to live the question. Perhaps you will gradually, without even noticing it, find yourself experiencing the answer, some distant day.'

RAINER MARIA RILKE

Exploring an Analogy

I like to think of a relationship as a work of art in progress; a sculpture in particular. Imagine you and your partner have a large block of marble in front of you. Out of this block of marble you are going to sculpt something wonderful and beautiful for both of you to enjoy. At the outset you are excited and motivated to get going, so you both start chipping away, except you didn't exactly decide on what the final piece would look like. Now you run into problems; it doesn't look as nice as you imagined and you lose motivation. Now one of you takes charge and the other follows instructions. It isn't exactly what either of you wanted but it's better than nothing. Soon you don't really enjoy looking at it because there is quite a lot of disappointment attached to the making of it.

Taking a Different View

That is one view of how it could be, but here's another view. You both stand in front of the block of marble. You have a rough picture of what you want to create, which one of you sketches out. You agree that it is what you are aiming for and that you will review what you are doing along the way, and get help when necessary. You agree that while you want it to be a lasting treasure, completion is not the goal; the measurement of success is to enjoy working on it and to feel that the time investment is worthwhile and purposeful. You recognize that creating the sculpture is not the only task you want to work on in your life so there may be periods where it is on hold. You recognize the same applies to your partner. So, sometimes you work on it together ensuring that enjoyment is a key priority; sometimes one of you is working on it alone within an agreed balance of creative licence and accountability and sometimes neither of you is working on it. It doesn't matter how long it takes because you never tire of it. It is crafted with loving attention and it represents both of you.

Take some time to imagine how this feels. Allow those feelings to permeate and notice the sensations throughout your body. If this is how you would like to feel in your relationship, ask the Universe to factor this in to your unconscious. There is nothing magical or complicated about this. Simply put the request out beyond yourself and allow your words to take on their own energy.

OLD COPING STRATEGIES

◆

When a relationship is floundering it is not unusual to find that needs such as respect, consideration, warmth, affection and understanding go unmet. If you have followed the process so far you should be able to call to mind a list of unmet needs for you and your partner. Are many of the unmet needs the same? It is interesting to notice how we compensate for unmet needs and how the coping strategies we use are often the least likely to get us what we really want.

ONE COPING STRATEGY that seems harmless enough is to find a peer group where we can receive agreement and empathy for our position. When a relationship isn't going well, one or both partners might gravitate towards friends and acquaintances who support positions such as 'all men are useless' or 'all women moan'. This may not be explicit, but these themes run as undercurrents in certain gatherings and they serve to hold us in a place that doesn't help our situation. However, because on some level we don't believe things can ever change, we find solace in such positions.

Many people think I was pursuing an unrealistic ideal in trying to find a partner who would enjoy learning how to build intimacy through skilful communication and apply it in a joint personal and professional venture. Even counsellors I have spoken to were convinced that I was pursuing something unattainable. I have been on the receiving end of many direct lectures and many indirect subtexts advising me that I was asking too much of life. And it has been painful to experience friends confirm their fears about me when I walked away from two marriages because I could not see a way to meet my needs in those relationships.

I perceived it differently. It seemed to me that some people I know had settled for substandard relationships and wanted me to join their club so that they could feel better about their own choices. And while this may perhaps be a rather arrogant perception on my part, I had questioned myself enough to realize that I would rather be on my own than not have the communication I yearned for in a relationship. That was my position. The position came from studying my perception.

Communication that Builds Safety

When David, my partner, agreed to enter into a relationship where we would learn how to communicate as part of a whole personal and professional lifestyle, he would be the first to admit that it was a lot easier said than done. It took us about two years to settle into something that worked and to get to the point where we could agree that this was a good relationship. We then created a genuinely safe space for us both where the conflict ethos is not about one person changing to suit the other; it is about realizing that even when just one of us is suffering we both need to step back, adjust and evaluate our positions, and change something together.

The Language of Needs & Feelings

There is real confusion about needs and feelings because of how we use the words. I have written such things as, 'You need to speak to your partner,' but I am not expressing a need; I am expressing a strategy to meet a need. The same applies to feelings. Any sentence that starts with, 'I feel like...' is unlikely to express a feeling. 'I feel like hitting him', is not an expression of a feeling, neither is 'I feel like running away'.

The feeling might be frustration, anger or fear. What has been expressed is a strategy that leapfrogs over the feelings and needs and goes straight into a solution. Going straight to solutions avoids ever having to truly experience the emotions. In doing that, we miss out the process of examination that builds foundations for more reliable outcomes.

It suddenly occurred to me that, since David is the person I share everything with and since he gets mentioned in this book several times, I should stop writing and consult him on these points. His comment in response to what I have written about our relationship is this: 'I know I am in a place of trust and love so whenever some tension or conflict arises as it invariably does in life, I have a set of tools that are easy to use, accessible, and help me to have the real conversation. The great thing is that it doesn't matter if our communication fails or breaks down in any one conversation; our process allows for as many attempts as it takes to sort it out without there being a crisis because the foundations that were laid in the beginning are solid and safe.'

His statement meets all my needs for mutuality, trust, love and understanding. I hope you will be able to see that when a couple has communication as powerful as this, anything is do-able because the dialogue opens doors. It then becomes possible to make realistic agreements about every issue.

COMPROMISE OR CHANGE

There is a very big difference between compromising on needs and changing the way we meet our needs. It is hard when other issues get in the way of contentment in a relationship. Obvious ones that come up are money and work but I'm not treating those as needs. They are satisfiers. Most clients come to see me because they are not content with their lives and they are frightened of the steps they would need to take to bring about the real change they seek.

ONE CLIENT IN PARTICULAR COMES TO MIND. Jon worked for a large corporate firm. Every week at his appointment he would tell me how awful his work was, how he disliked his boss and how he had ideas for running his own business. The only thing stopping him was money. He would

not be able to afford to stay in his house and run his car if he left his job. It was clear that he was meeting needs for security and structure without realizing that this was at a complete cost to creativity and freedom.

Once I had understood and empathized with Jon's position, I asked him the following question: 'I guess you come to see me because you like the support, but I'm confused about the kind of support you want. Do you want me to help you recognize and accept the choices you make so that you can find happiness in your job and life the way it is now, or do you want me to help you recognize and accept the choices that you make to enable you to make changes?'

It is a really important question, and you need to know your position in relation to that question if you are trying to talk with your partner. The nature of my work with individuals and couples makes that question important because it determines the nature of the support that is needed. For many people the decision to change the external landscape is simply a response to continuing discomfort.

You need to ask yourself if you are trying to find contentment with how things are or if you are trying to change an external trigger. Are you trying to change an external trigger in order to continue to support a perception or position that is no longer serving you? For example, do you look for a new job whenever you feel uncomfortable at work, or do you work out what needs to change inside you so that you can be

content with what you have? Looking for a new job is simply changing the external trigger. Without some internal work you are likely to encounter the same problems.

Exploring Needs

If you don't understand what it is that you are doing – how your thoughts and feelings are translating into your behaviours and actions – you need to consider how another person can support you. Of course, in a therapeutic setting, it is my job to help my clients explore this and find their own answers. In a relationship you need to have some clarity, or at least know that you don't have clarity because your partner is not a mind reader or your counsellor and cannot tell you what your unmet needs are.

Every time you are uncomfortable in a relationship, do you look for external things to change? And do you end up feeling the same way again after all the activity has ended? This is why differentiating needs from satisfiers is so important. If you are fixed on a particular satisfier being the only answer to your happiness then you limit your creativity for finding alternative strategies that will meet your needs. For even more clarity on needs, it is important to understand that I am speaking about needs such as those described in Abraham Maslow's book, *Motivation and Personality*. I am not talking about needs in the way a nurse or social worker might do a Needs Assessment and calculate that you need a walking aid.

Speaking about needs creates equality because we can all recognize needs for ourselves and each other. My need isn't any more or less important than your need, so if you tell me your need is respect, I recognize the need and I would like you to have that need met. If you ask me to help, I probably will. If you try to meet your need for respect by attempting to dominate me, I will walk away if I can or submit with resentment because, in trying to meet your own need, you have not taken into consideration my need for choice.

Unspoken Contracts & Compromises

When a relationship begins and we are both behaving at our absolute best we make many unspoken contracts and compromises. These set up a certain way of being together. After a while it becomes difficult to live up to the 'best possible you', so you start dismantling the contracts through actions rather than renegotiation. This is when problems may emerge.

I remember a particular client, James, who wanted to find out why his relationships never worked out. He was good-looking, solvent and had a good sense of humour. Every time he met a girl he would shower her with attention, giving her flowers, gifts and taking her to dinner at lovely restaurants. He would pay attention to her likes and dislikes by, for example, playing her favourite music in his car when he picked her up. Soon he would start taking on DIY or other practical tasks for her. It all sounded wonderful. I can imagine most girls feeling very elated at being paid so much attention by such an eligible man and, on some level, this chivalry feeds some archetypal beliefs about men as providers.

In reality, James just wanted to be liked. Being liked was more important than anything else, so he presented himself in a way that was pretty much guaranteed to make this happen. The truth is that James found all that giving quite traumatic so, at the point where he had gained the girl's trust and favour, he would let go of doing quite so much. Bit by bit he would start becoming resentful, wondering why the girl never did anything for him and then he would begin acting differently; he would be late for dates or even just cancel them.

Having set the relationship up with himself as the giver and the girl as the receiver he had made an unspoken contract. Of course, some relationships never got off the ground because some girls found the disproportionate amount of giving to be off-putting. So the girls attracted to him would be those who preferred receiving to giving. And, of course this would be unsustainable on any long-term basis, since giving and receiving are like breathing – they need to be balanced.

Unspoken Contracts

You might like to think about any unspoken contracts that you and your partner may have set up and how one or both of you may be trying to challenge the contract without any real dialogue. This reminds me of a situation I once experienced

in a conference call. One person on the call assumed the role of a facilitative leader. This person, a friend of mine, is known for her expertise as a facilitator and I have much admiration for her skills and qualities.

In a previous conference call she had been called upon to be the facilitator, and somehow, in inviting her to do it once, we had all made an unspoken contract that this would remain her role. Her ability to slip into the role with ease and confidence made it possible for the situation to go unnoticed. I eventually did question the situation and it led to a very connecting conversation about how leadership roles protect us from insecurity and are, in fact, a way of making a situation emotionally safe.

A fixed position is usually a response to other positions and an attempt to find power when you feel powerless.

We explored a little about taking a position earlier in the book when I asked you to consider your own position. When you adopt a position, it is in relation to your environment and the positions of other people. If you were the only person ever to exist on the planet, your position, if you could create one at all, would be very different to the position you have now. A fixed position is usually a response to other positions and an attempt to find power when you feel powerless, and the more powerless you feel the more fixed you become.

POWER STRUGGLES

◆

Once you experience disappointment in a relationship, you uncon-
sciously use power struggles to get your needs met. Many experts will
tell you that the power struggle is a natural stage of a relationship.
I don't agree with this opinion. I believe our education system pro-
vided us with collective beliefs that perpetuate a state of struggle.

A POWER STRUGGLE IS, in fact, a competition to see if we can get our partner to meet the needs that we have been unable to meet ourselves. If we lived in a society where exploring needs and experiencing feelings were an integral part of our education system, this competition would not arise. Many couples remain locked in a power struggle until one or both concedes and settles for a compromise. Many relationships will break down during the power struggle phase, which is a shame as it provides the perfect opportunity for learning about how to meet our needs.

Finding a balance between autonomy and intimacy can be the source of a power struggle. We all need both yet every relationship must find its own balance; there is no 'one-size-fits-all' formula. It takes time and practice to find what works and, even then, challenges and opportunities will continuously present themselves and alter the landscape against which you decided your balance. This is a fluid place. The tide ebbs and flows and the sands change and shift. Flexibility is the key.

REFLECTIONS

As this chapter comes to an end I hope you have experienced a mixture of feelings as you read through the propositions. I fully expect that you will have enjoyed some parts more than others and maybe even felt some irritation or overwhelmed in other parts. This doesn't matter. Your subconscious will take whatever it wants and put it into the mix. The various subjects were simply doorways and you will have intuitively known which doors had your name on them without you having to consciously do anything.

Now, you can begin to call back the reflections from your subconscious. Breathe and relax. Go back to the self-healing and self-energizing exercise and take yourself through the process: relaxing, breathing, grounding and opening to the light. Honour yourself and your commitment to this journey. Celebrate that you have done your groundwork and really engage with the idea of 'waking up' to life and giving every moment your full attention so that you can truly be alive. Have confidence that the time and energy you have invested in this will show itself as having been worthwhile in the next phases of the journey.

CHAPTER FIVE

AUTHENTIC DIALOGUE

*Being authentic is directly linked to the level
of self-reflection and honesty you have within yourself.
Authenticity is something you reach and find within
yourself. When you become authentic, you find a
genuine place of love and respect. So what do we mean
by 'authentic dialogue'? 'Authentic' means a sense of
actuality without untruths or misrepresentation.
'Dialogue' is an exchange of ideas and thoughts
on a particular issue with a view to reaching
an amicable agreement.*

MOVING FORWARD WITH YOUR PARTNER

◆

To have any kind of dialogue there needs to be more than one person present so this chapter requires you and your partner to join in. Earlier in the book, I mentioned that this process is aimed at those who are starting a relationship, those who want to improve an existing relationship or those who feel stuck where they are. Whatever your circumstance, dialogue is the way forward.

I F YOU READ THE QUOTE on the opposite page from the teachings of the Dalai Lama, you might be wondering how the history of wars has anything to do with relationships. I wrote earlier about things that are taught to us being promoted as the natural way of things. One idea that comes out of old thinking is to see people we are in conflict with as an enemy. So when we get into conflict with our partner, suddenly the person who we sleep with and with whom we share food and resources becomes an enemy who is attacking us.

I see this old thinking demonstrated everywhere. When a student in school doesn't act in harmony with the values of the adults, they become an enemy to be coerced into compliance. When a worker doesn't follow the norms of the workplace, they will become an enemy that needs to be punished. I see examples all the time where there is no real dialogue going on; just lots of rhetoric and posturing. Without real dialogue there is little hope of change.

The History of Wars

'War seems to be part of the history of humanity. As we look at the situation of our planet in the past, countries, regions and even villages were economically independent of one another. Under those circumstances, the destruction of our enemy might have been a victory for us. There was a relevance to violence and war. However, today we are so interdependent that the concept of war has become out dated. When we face problems or disagreements today, we have to arrive at solutions through dialogue. Dialogue is the only appropriate method.'

FROM 'AN OPEN HEART: PRACTICING COMPASSION IN EVERYDAY LIFE',
BY THE DALAI LAMA
LITTLE, BROWN & COMPANY, 2001

When I first read this teaching by the Dalai Lama I was struck by how much it resonated with me. It occurred to me that we have maintained this pattern of war within our relationships because this is the example we have been set. We strive to win each argument – to win the battle. Consider how many battles you have fought and how much energy you have thrown away on things that really didn't matter. That's not to say we should submit or put aside our own thoughts and feelings; but what we need to find is a compassionate method of standing our ground while hearing the other person. Authentic dialogue provides this method.

Being Authentic

At the beginning of this book, I put you on a voyage of self-discovery in order to get to actuality rather than untruths or misrepresentation. I'm not suggesting that you deliberately gave a false or misrepresented view at the beginning; but if we had worked through one-to-one sessions together, we would now be comparing what you presented as your truth when you started and seeing how it is different from your truth after examination and reflection.

The problem has not changed, but your understanding of the problem will have evolved. So often we dive into conversations based on perceptions which we tell ourselves is our 'gut instinct'. I wonder how much 'gut instinct' keeps you stuck in a cycle of experiencing the world from this one position? Because even if you don't like this position, at least it is familiar and you know who you are and how you might respond. We can be change-resistant to the point where we repeat things we know to be unhealthy without consideration.

I will always challenge clients who tell me that their gut instinct is their guiding principle. I ask them to think of a dozen concrete examples of their 'gut instinct' being right over a period of time, so as to get them to recognize that gut instinct is only one tool in a range of skills and senses we use to guide us. It is very easy to forget the times we had a 'gut instinct' in which our fears were not realized and we had made an incorrect assumption about a person or situation.

Gaining Awareness of Authenticity

I once worked with a couple who needed some changes in their relationship: Adam had accused his partner Mary of constantly putting him down. Mary claimed that she was expressing her likes and dislikes equally as she went along and that Adam would only hear the negative and never the positive. Over time, Adam learned that, on the whole, Mary expressed more gratitude and delight in the things he did than dissatisfaction and disappointment. However, Adam's 'gut instinct' – his position – was that everything he did was wrong so, of course, he could only hear those examples of when he'd done wrong. It reaffirmed his position.

To make a change he had to become alive to the full extent of the relationship rather than alert to just the parts that suited his position. After Mary made some slight adjustments to her choice of language and timings, Adam was able to make a shift. So authenticity in this context involved going beyond his reactions and discomfort and into a deeper state of awareness.

Dialogue vs. Debate

A dialogue is defined as a very specific type of open-ended conversation in which the cornerstones are collaboration and goodwill. The aim of dialogue is to decide a way forward that works for everyone, based on common ground. A debate, on the other hand, is a form of competition where the participants put their best idea or proposal forward and try to get everyone on their side. No matter how polite the conversation is, and how many gracious manners are displayed, if the intention is to impose a view on someone else, it is a debate.

When I ask my grown-up children to help with the cleaning and they don't, I continue trying to get them to do my bidding. But no matter how polite I am there is no dialogue taking place. I am making a demand through a debate; not making a request through a dialogue. And, not surprisingly, when I am imposing my demands on another person (even in my most compelling way), I might win the immediate battle but the war still rages.

I am not interested in engaging in a war with anyone when a dialogue will work better, so this has taught me to find another way. I don't want to see people as enemies and I don't enjoy battles. Dialogue appears to take longer because everyone's contribution needs to be heard and understood; however, I discovered that once dialogue is established and embedded as the way forward, it is a very quick process, which provides lasting results and cooperative relationships. And, because it is fulfilling and enjoyable, it doesn't matter that it takes longer because the process is as important as the outcome.

Once everyone has had their voice heard, agreements are voluntary and heartfelt. By using dialogue I can be safe in the knowledge that resentments will not be leaking out in other battles. Once you choose dialogue as your path you develop a compassionate shorthand for discussing topics. You trust its

authenticity and you know that the foundations are safe and solid. In this way mutuality builds, intimacy grows and the dialogues are quicker.

Combining 'authentic' and 'dialogue' results in a very powerful formula in which we listen to each other's inner truths so that together we can find a shared truth. We then use the shared truth to inform our decisions.

PRESENTING YOUR INNER TRUTH

So how are you going to present your inner truth in your relationship? It is a courageous and scary thing to do if you are not used to doing this. Showing our emotional vulnerability may make us fear rejection. But once you become accustomed to doing it, it will become a way of life and the basis of self-confidence.

THERE ARE RISKS IN PRESENTING YOUR INNER TRUTH, such as having your truth minimized or dismissed rendering you vulnerable. Of course, in a debate you would never display vulnerability because it leaves you open to attack, so the idea of being vulnerable in a conversation might seem counter-intuitive. However, part of our collective truth as humans is vulnerability. We are all vulnerable. At its most obvious we are continuously physically vulnerable; at any moment a natural disaster could hit.

Debate & Dialogue

Debate is about opposing.
Dialogue is about collaboration.

Debate is competitive to win an argument.
Dialogue is collaborative to find common ground.

Debate is not concerned with feelings.
Dialogue is sensitive to feelings.

Debate looks for flaws and faults in the other's proposition.
Dialogue looks for the best parts of a proposition.

Debate is about defending one's own ideas.
Dialogue is about being open to improvements.

Debate encourages criticism of others.
Dialogue encourages evaluation of self.

Debate presents for either/or choices.
Dialogue opens as many choices as possible.

Debate highlights difference.
Dialogue highlights agreements.

Debate tries to impose a solution.
Dialogue is continuously open to new solutions.

Emotional Vulnerability

Less obvious is emotional vulnerability, where we are scared of displaying our vulnerability because we fear attack or rejection. But one of the reasons for being in a relationship is to find intimacy. To be intimate requires us to share our vulnerabilities. When we have sex, we are at our most vulnerable at the point of orgasm. In fact, it is an ultimate point of vulnerability because, if you want to have an orgasm, you must give way and yield to it. Now for a minute or two focus on that moment of surrender and the sense of yielding to it. If you have stopped having sex in your relationship, there are many emotional reasons surrounding power struggles that can be explored, but you have also denied yourself an important place of vulnerability. That's a very tough way to live since we are all vulnerable and expressing it is part of being alive.

But, as in any situation in which we take risks, it is important to use discretion. Just as we calculate risk when making ourselves physically vulnerable, to discuss emotional vulnerabilities we need to create the conditions in which we are most likely to have our inner truth heard and respected.

Creating the Conditions for Dialogue

If you have been the leader of this process, this is where it all changes. Now you need the cooperation of your partner. Your partner needs to understand what is happening, why it is happening and what the outcomes could be. Once again,

◆

'The true spirit of conversation consists in building on
another man's observation, not overturning it.'

EDWARD BULWER-LYTTON

◆

---

it will be helpful if you pick a good moment to let your partner know that you would like to have a further discussion
about the relationship.

Remember that it is always a good idea to ask permission
before springing something on someone. This is how I might
approach a discussion: 'Is this a good time to run something
by you?' Assuming it is, or I have come back at an appointed
time, I might say: 'Since we had that chat about your feelings,
I've had some time to reflect on it all and I'd like to have
another conversation. How does that sound to you?'

Avoiding an Ambush

Every time you speak you are creating a set of conditions for
a response. In this case you want to create the conditions in
which you will engage your partner to willingly participate
in a compassionate conversation, but if you spring something
on someone without asking permission or giving them time
to prepare, it can be perceived as an ambush. An ambush puts
people into panic mode because it forces them to start risk
assessing for danger, so you are not likely to get the same
response as when a person feels relaxed and comfortable.

My partner David and I have lots of conversational short-hands that have been founded out of dialogue. One of them is an accepted 'not now', where each of us understands that this is not a good time to get full attention. We both trust that there is no rejection or disapproval involved and that no explanation is needed. It is simply a signal to find a better time. Even so, I have been very used to being a decision-maker for most of my life and now I often fall into the trap of making decisions on the spot. While it is a good skill to have, it is actually quite stressful, so I allow myself to take some time whenever I can. David, on the other hand, was taught to defer decisions and look for any danger or consequences before committing to anything. That makes us a very interesting combination, with him on the brake and me on the accelerator. It is therefore obvious that we need to create the conditions in which we can make joint decisions where I am happy to slow down a bit and he is happy to speed up a bit.

Preparing the Space

Once you have established that you are both willing participants in the dialogue, you can decide on the time and place. Prepare the space where you will talk. Adjust the lighting and the ambiance of the room and ensure you have privacy. Now the scene has been set. You both know you are going to have a dialogue and you are both as relaxed and comfortable as you can be with each other.

What are you going to talk about and how are you going to talk about it? I can't tell you that – it is your life; but I am simply asking you to open your heart and immerse yourself in the dialogue. I can offer some topics to get you started. Later on in the chapter are some pointers on how best to have the conversation.

SAFETY IN A RELATIONSHIP

◆

A good starting point for a dialogue is safety. How safe is this relationship? Depending on the state of your relationship this might be a short or long discussion. If you know the relationship is solid and there is no threat, then this discussion is simply an affirmation. If you are not so sure, then this is a serious discussion point. It is really difficult to have any kind of mutuality if there is even a subtle threat to the relationship because the partner under threat does not know how to plan or what to plan for.

S O MANY RELATIONSHIPS ARE BASED on a power imbalance, where one person holds an implied threat over the other which, if loosely put into words, would read like this: 'If you don't conform to the standards I set, or if you take me out of my comfort zone more times than I can tolerate, then I will dump you after doing things that I know will make you feel the same level of pain that you inflict on me.' The showdown

comes when the threatened partner says, 'OK, leave then, it's over' and the threatening partner realizes he or she had no intention of carrying out the threat. It was intended to do two things: to motivate the threatened partner into compliance and provide a licence for sabotaging behaviour. This strategy can hold a couple in a very unhappy place for years.

Let's look at the other side of that coin where one partner gets compliance to a set of demands. The reason for making those demands is that they have found it hard to trust others and they believe that setting rules will bring them safety. In reality, the demanding partner will never truly know whether the compliant partner is doing it out of freedom or out of fear. This actually increases insecurity and therefore exacerbates the problem.

A demanding partner has a lot of self-awareness work to do in learning how to trust and how to live with disappointment. Waking up is about realizing that behind the rules and demands is a person with unmet needs, trying to get help.

Understanding Relationships

The following explanation is what I believe is at the heart of relationships in terms of the balance of power: 'It is true that sometimes I will want you to do things for me and I have all sorts of skilful means in which I can persuade you to do them: I have ways of turning up the volume and the pressure so I can achieve what I want. But if you do anything because you have been coerced or motivated by fear, guilt or shame, then no human transaction of any real value has taken place between us. Before you do anything for me, I want you to be sure that you are doing it voluntarily and with a good heart. And if when you check inside yourself the answer is 'no', I would really like to understand because this tells me some important information about you. We can then process it as a couple and find a mutual 'yes' that works for both of us.'

Dealing with Crisis

It will be difficult to conduct any relationship that does not feel safe. If the relationship is in crisis, it is good to set a timeframe for exploration and dialogue where both of you agree to put the conflict down and do some work. When couples come to me in crisis not knowing if they want to separate, I usually advise that we do six sessions at two-weekly intervals as an exploration. At the end, we review what we have learned and the couple can make an informed decision about their future.

Most couples want to save their relationship and then we begin a process of regular sessions with the intention of strengthening the relationship. Of course, some couples do decide to break up and we then use the sessions to organize a separation or divorce with the least amount of suffering. Occasionally, a couple reaches a point where one wants to split and the other wants to hold on. More exploration is needed in order for them to make a decision.

Letting Go

One family I worked with was caught in a situation like this; we'll call the parents Jake and Clare. Jake had already moved out of the family home. Clare could not accept that the relationship was over. We did eighteen months of monthly sessions until Clare finally accepted what had happened. The outcome did not bring the couple together but without the sessions they would have been at war for much longer, spent a fortune on legal fees and Jake would have ended up taking out an injunction against Clare, leaving a lifetime of emotional consequences for their six-year-old daughter.

EXPLORING THE PAST

Another good topic for your dialogue is the past and what has gone before. It is important to go over what has happened so that you can let go of old resentments and find forgiveness. We expect to be happy, but relationships can be full of disappointments when expectations we believe were actually our rights go unfulfilled.

WHEN YOU WENT INTO YOUR RELATIONSHIP, perhaps you imagined that you would always feel happy rather than sad. Did you go into a relationship hoping to find some sort of protection from sad feelings? I think most of us do until we learn the joy of being mindful of our feelings.

If the past contains a catalogue of incidents that trigger pain it is good to go over what happened in the past and admit any mistakes. Both you and your partner will be able to talk about what could have been said or done differently while recognizing the circumstances that contributed to the incident. You can use these explorations as learning for how you might conduct yourselves in the future.

Past Mistakes

Admitting past mistakes can be more difficult than it seems. We have been taught that mistakes are failures and as such, are shameful, and this usually triggers guilt. But all situations in life are unique, even if they seem repetitive. In any situation, you may not be entering with exactly the same circumstances, amount of knowledge or in the same emotional state as before. This means the potential is always there to make mistakes.

Even so, admitting mistakes is hard, especially if you confuse admitting a mistake with being at fault and taking blame. But when you avoid your true feelings and live a staged existence, life is unfulfilling; it is only safe if you never take risks or follow your heart. You might have been taught that admitting a mistake means submitting to another person. This might mean giving them the power to punish as we are told that this is the only system of organizing people that works.

An example of this happened to my daughter, who was 15 years old at the time. She asked to leave school early and at

AUTHENTIC DIALOGUE

the appointed time, not wanting to disrupt the class, she truly believed she had caught the teacher's eye and received a 'nod' to leave. On her return the next day and, in what felt like an ambush, she was summoned by the head teacher to receive a punishment for walking out of a lesson without permission.

She asked a simple question; 'When do I get to say what happened?' They told her she didn't have such an opportunity and that she had to accept a punishment because it was a consequence of what she did. She explained very simply. 'Well, I'll do whatever it is you're punishing me with, but I am going to find it very odd because I come from a home where we talk about things that happen, so I'm not sure what the point is here. I simply made a mistake.'

Learning from Mistakes

Admitting mistakes is a learning territory. Whatever has happened in the past cannot be changed; the clock cannot be turned back. The best that can happen now is a dialogue where mistakes are admitted and harm is repaired. This is a reality that both of you must come to in order to take self-responsibility and discuss who owns which part of the past. Once you have managed to do this, the next task is to mourn. This is where you remember the actions that you now regret and connect to the feelings and unmet needs you are experiencing in the present about them. This is a very important part of any moving-on process.

Hopes, Fears & Dreams

◆

*Your hopes, fears and dreams are another good topic for dialogue.
It is helpful first to understand your motivators and work out if they
are fear-driven or trust-driven. If you are fear-driven, then whenever something bad happens you adjust your life by minimizing risk
so as to avoid the negative emotions that come with bad experiences.*

I WAS IN THE PRESENCE OF A VERY WEALTHY ENTREPRENEUR
and he admitted that his success was driven by a fear of
failure. Continuously being good at his job and completely
ahead of the game ensured that he never had to experience
the pain of his family telling him he was a loser. This had happened once in his life when he had made a costly mistake in
the family business. Now his success was fear-driven.

If you are trust-driven, you allow life to happen and you do
not self-protect out of fear. That is not to say that you don't
use discretion – when it is used skilfully, this is a fit-for-pur-
pose tool – but when you live in trust, you know that things
go wrong and you have confidence in your resources to deal
with whatever presents itself.

Working out the Details

Generally our hopes, fears and dreams are abstract: 'I hope I
will be happy; I fear that I will end up destitute; I dream of
being in a loving relationship with a happy-ever-after ending.'

These are big, unspecific visions. They are a good starting point but will not suffice in designing a relationship without detail. Details are very important in a relationship because everything matters and the sooner we deal with the tensions or conflicts that arise, the easier they are to work out.

Working out details can be a murky territory because if we confuse detail with trivia it becomes easy for one partner to dismiss the other partner's niggle as trivial and controlling. In fact, the person doing the dismissing is doing all the controlling. He or she is determining what subjects can and cannot be broached and setting the level at which a problem becomes important enough to deal with. Discussing our hopes, fears and dreams also helps us to set the agenda for a deeper discussion, which includes subjects like, 'Where do we see this relationship in five or ten years time?', 'What would we do if…' and, 'How shall we manage a particular situation?'

Guidelines for Dialogue

Remember the scene has been set and the conditions created for some relaxed time together. Here are some guidelines that can be helpful as a framework for dialogue:

• The roles of listener and speaker are identified.

• In the role of speaker, you are responsible for what you say and how you say it. You should have some literacy around feelings and needs and avoid casting blame. You should indicate to the listener when you have finished speaking.

• In the role of listener, you are only there to receive the other person. It should be without opinion, judgement, criticism or blame. Check the speaker has completed what he or she wants to say before replying. Any response you give is to show that you have heard and understood. Do this by repeating back what you have heard. Any questions you ask are only there for the purpose of clarity.

• These roles are interchangeable as long as it is explicit that it is happening. The speaker must agree that he or she is finished for the time being or can complete later.

• The speaker and listener will not interrupt each other.

• Whatever you hear or express, resist the urge to fix it at this stage. Just allow it all to be in its fullest form.

• Agree that if either of you sense any pressure, tension, frustration or impatience, that you will take a short break and return to the conversation. Alternatively, you could agree a wind-up time and a date to resume the dialogue.

• Speak in a calm voice and remain seated and relaxed.

• Nothing said in the dialogue can be used or referred to outside of agreed discussion times until both of you agree that the dialogue is completed and you are both satisfied.

• Agree that any distractions and interruptions like the phone will be diverted or ignored for a set period.

• If one or both of you breaks an agreed guideline, resist the urge to blame; notice it, admit to it and work out what might help to keep within the guidelines.

If you haven't entered into dialogue before, allow yourself several attempts to get it right. Don't expect your partner to suddenly start speaking calmly if he or she usually raises their voice or that you will suddenly be able to remain silent if you have a culture of interruption in the relationship. And don't use the inability to get the dialogue right as an excuse to blame your partner for not joining in properly.

Go back to the intention, which is engagement. If you get engagement, say thank you, even if it is not the engagement you imagined. You both need to be willing to move forward. Punishing your partner for not performing well will diminish any willingness to try again.

REFLECTIONS

As you make your attempts at authentic dialogue, it is worth going over what happened in each attempt.

- What went well?
- What went badly?
- What did you discover?
- How has the dialogue changed any of your perceptions or positions?
- What's your level of enthusiasm for doing more to improve the relationship?

CHAPTER SIX

THE WAY FORWARD

By now you have had an authentic dialogue. It may have taken several attempts but you have both now really discovered and explored your togetherness. After all the talking is over you will want to actually put some change into action. There is still some practical work to be done. A cornerstone of a functioning relationship is the quality of the agreements you make together and how you uphold them.

Identifying Strategies

◆

If you have followed this process fully then you will have a real grasp of the needs you and you partner are both trying to meet and a sense of the loss associated with unmet needs. You will both have given each other empathy and understanding and will now be in possession of the full extent of the state of your relationship and where it is heading if it stays on this trajectory.

As a result of the conversation you have had with your partner, you will now probably want to change some things. Now you can begin to identify strategies for the way forward. If you have understood this book in the way I intended, it will be obvious why I asked you to do so much groundwork before deciding on a strategy. My guess is the strategies you would have chosen prior to doing this work are different to the strategies you choose now. Before doing the foundation work, you might have dreamed up strategies without too much consultation with your partner. Your partner, in turn, might have been busy drawing up strategies that were likely to collide with yours.

Working on Strategies

The strategies you agree upon must be realistic and do-able. This means that you can actually do the tasks in the agreement within the parameters that are set. If you set yourselves a big

goal, don't forget to do the detail on the little steps that will get you there. I can't tell you what these strategies might be; they are what create your unique coupledom, but the acid test is to hold them up against the needs you are trying to meet.

There are no rights and wrongs about any strategy you choose. Your family and friends will all have their own opinions, which might not concur with your own. Just remember that a strategy that involves more than one person contains agreements to take actions and, as long as the agreements have been made voluntarily, with a good heart and are open to review, you are on the right track. It is important that the agreements are understood in detail and contain things such as who is doing what and by when, for how long and what a positive outcome looks like.

About Agreements

In order to make an agreement you need to generate options. These options will be based on all the exploration and discovery you did with each other. You will need to work through this process together. The right attitude is to think, 'Yes, and' instead of, 'No, but'.

To get into the mood, try this really simple improvisational game. Start with a fun idea or event, for example, 'Yesterday, I went for a picnic with my friend'. The other person says, 'No, but...' and adds another piece to the story for example, 'No, but it started to rain so we took cover under some trees,'

Relationships & Agreements

To be successful, a relationship has three main ingredients, which act as the headings for everything else: unconditional love, conditional agreements and trust.

Unconditional love is being alive to the well-being of another person with no thought to personal gain. Therefore, when things go wrong, we do not withdraw our love or withhold our care; in fact we go out of our way to help.

Conditional agreements are a set of negotiated terms. We agree to live by these terms, which are arrived at voluntarily.

Trust is reliance and confidence in yourself, your partner and the relationship so that you can predict how you and your partner will be in various situations.

At the end of the book (see pages 140–141), you will find a sample relationship contract, which you might use as a starting point for a discussion.

and you both continue adding a 'No, but' until you give up. The story should get quite ridiculous.

Now try the same exercise with 'Yes, and' so the response to 'Yesterday, I went for a picnic with my friend' might be 'Yes, and she invited all our old school friends'. Notice the difference in energy levels and where the stories lead.

Formulating Ideas

Ask yourselves what you would most like to happen in your relationship; what you hope to achieve. Use a brainstorming format and write the ideas up on separate pieces of paper.

- Generate as many ideas as possible and remove limits.
- Don't criticize any idea; concentrate on extending or building on the idea.
- Be creative with unusual ideas by suspending limitations and assumptions.
- Improve the ideas by combining them.

Now summarize the options and stretch yourselves to find more ideas. Try putting these into an order of first choice, second choice etc. If you get stuck, ask your subconscious to work it out then leave it and come back to it another time. When you're ready, start assessing the options using some or all of these filters.

- Do the agreements satisfy feelings and needs both in the long and short term?
- Are they fair and have you both participated fully?
- Do they promote a better relationship?
- Do you have the resources, energy and commitment to make it happen?
- Do you understand what is required of you to make it happen?
- What's the timescale?
- How will success be measured?

- When will you review your progress?
- What could be gained or lost by not using this solution?
- Could this option have any unintended consequences?
- What will the outcome be if either one of you breaks the agreement?

Looking Towards Positive Outcomes

The whole purpose of this exercise is for you to be able to change your relationship in a considered and thoughtful way, where you both feel equally that your stake in the outcome is important and valued and will benefit both of you.

Having made agreements, you will want them to manifest into positive outcomes. Imagine the outcomes that you want and sense the feelings that will come with these positive outcomes. If what you want is more quality time together, then imagine the feelings that go with having achieved that and tune into those feelings, spending some time talking about them.

Remember, it is not a business meeting; it is a process of intimacy building which requires loving care, compassionate language and proper planning. There is an accepted myth that relationships should be spontaneous and impromptu. Built into that myth is the belief that if our partners loved us, they would instinctively know what would please us.

To get to spontaneity, there needs to be some serious effort put into truly knowing each other. When you really know each other, you will develop a shorthand that will be the spring-

board for instinctive actions that are well received. I recall a conversation with a client who was unhappy in her relationship:

ME: *'What would you like to have in your relationship that is not there now?'*

CLIENT: *'I don't know.'*

ME: *'That's an interesting answer.'*

CLIENT: *'How come?'*

ME: *'You have spent some time letting me know how unhappy you are in your relationship and that you cannot identify the source of your unhappiness. I wonder if something else is going on here? I believe we have been taught not to be needy and, if we do have some unmet needs, whatever happens we mustn't tell anyone. I also believe that if we choose to live like that we can expect to feel miserable so I interpret your "I don't know" as embarrassment for needing something.'*

CLIENT: *'Well, I'm not asking for the moon. I just want him to be more romantic.'*

ME: *'That depends on what you mean by "be more romantic". Romantic to you might be bringing you the moon.'*

CLIENT: *'What do you mean?'*

ME: *'Well, if you asked me to be more romantic, I would have no idea what you expected me to do, so I might do nothing rather than risk getting it wrong.'*

CLIENT: *'I never thought of it like that.'*

ME: *'Yes, it's important to make clear requests because if we are not clear about what we want to happen, think how hard it is for another person to interpret our needs.'*

CLIENT: *'OK, so now I get the idea but I'm not sure how I could ask for what I'm thinking of.'*

ME: *'Well try it out on me.'*

CLIENT: *'What I really want is for him to guess what I want before I ask for it.'*

ME: *'How realistic is that?'*

CLIENT: *'Not at all.'*

ME: *'So how about we explore some more do-able ways that he could demonstrate being romantic and how about we involve him in this conversation so that he can participate in any agreements.'*

CLIENT: *'Sounds like a plan.'*

In the sessions that followed we discovered that my client's partner felt powerless in the relationship because he sensed her dissatisfaction but didn't know what to do about it. She was able to articulate some simple requests, such as having two minutes to embrace before getting out of bed. He was happy to agree to these, especially as they didn't involve going to the moon!

SELF-HEALING & SELF-ENERGIZING EXERCISE

◆

After an agreement-making conversation, go back to the self-healing and self-energizing exercise. This time you are going to do it together. Again, find a comfortable space. Prepare the room with incense and put on some soft, dreamy instrumental music. Find some cushions and sit on the floor facing each other close enough to hold hands.

1. Once you are seated and ready, make eye contact with each other and place your hands out to each other with one hand palm up and the other palm down and get your partner to touch hands with you palm to palm. Make a declaration of your commitment and love in whatever way works for you. Keep it simple and heartfelt. Then close your eyes and imagine a stream of light coming from above and encompassing you both. Sit in the light together and breathe. Bring your breathing right down to a slow, relaxed rhythm. Just be in the moment. When the time seems right, one of you will lie on your back and assume the role of receiver and the other will kneel alongside and assume the role of giver. If kneeling or lying flat isn't comfortable or possible find a position that works for both of you.

2. Now as the giver place one hand on your partner's forehead and the other on your partner's tummy just below the belly button and ask them to relax and breathe. At the same time, imagine your heart opening and sending pure love energy to your partner. Remember that there is no magic formula. Just by imagining it, it is done. If you find yourself distracted by thoughts, notice them and watch them pass like a cloud moving through the sky and just return your focus to the heart's energy. Spend as long as is comfortable doing this. Now move to your partner's head and place your hands very gently at either side of their face over the temples away from the eyes. Stay in that position, close your eyes and go to your garden of contentment. Remember that your partner's garden was backing onto yours. Now redesign both gardens into one big space where you are both content.

3. In a spirit of ease and delight, enjoy the creative process by designing a harmonious garden that works for both of you. Bask in the joy and spend some time walking around the garden together enjoying your space. Bring in the sculpture that you were imagining in Chapter Four and place it at the centre of the garden. If your mind wanders, just notice it and return to the garden.

4. When you are ready, let go and move down to your partner's feet. Find a comfortable position and hold their feet. Allow yourself to remember all the reasons why you entered into the relationship and think of five qualities that you like in your partner. Remember the times when your partner displayed those qualities. When you are complete, place your palms together and give gratitude for all that you have. Gently squeeze your partner's hand and ask them to swap places. Now repeat the ritual in reversed roles.

Working Towards Harmony

Once the two of you can relax into this place together, you will begin to notice a shift. I am not saying any of this is easy. To get here, I fully expect there will have been a few false

starts and some frustration. Remember that when you feel frustration and disappointment, it says more about you than it does about your partner. It is like an art exhibition or theatrical show. When you give your opinion, it says more about you than it does about the artist.

REFLECTIONS

Throughout the book you have been working towards equilibrium. You have balanced the inhalation and exhalation of breathing, you have been the listener and the speaker and you have been the giver and the receiver. You have been experiencing complementary forces and practising being comfortable in either energy. You have swapped roles with your partner in order to broaden understanding, sharing and cooperation. And you have made agreements as a building block to the solid foundations of your relationship. Contracts and agreements are simply a passport to a stronger bond. The aim is to build a bond that can withstand life's disturbances.

Ask yourself:

- What do I most enjoy about giving?
- What do I most enjoy about receiving?
- How does making and keeping agreements contribute to my well-being?

CHAPTER SEVEN

MAINTENANCE

*You will want to be able to go about
your everyday business safe in the knowledge that
you are both honouring your relationship and
respecting the agreements you have made. When you
reach this place, upholding and maintaining your
relationship will be joyful. But it is important to
keep the relationship alive. With a little imagination
there are lots of ways you can remind your partner
you love him or her, but without regular
maintenance these actions might not be
received as well as you would hope.*

UPHOLDING YOUR RELATIONSHIP

◆

I hope I have shared with you a purposeful journey that you can continue to revisit. Here I am assuming that the journey is now second nature, that you have mastered the navigation visiting all the twists and turns and that you can do it blindfolded.

I MAGINE THAT YOU AND YOUR PARTNER went through the whole project management process of building a house, taking on different roles and responsibilities and reporting back to each other. Now, you want to live in the house. The investment you have made holds a lot of meaning for you so you want to be sure it pays off. Living in the house should be enjoyable but there are some ongoing tasks such as maintenance and cleaning that you will need to do in order to keep the place in an enjoyable state and protect your investment.

◆

'None of us can exist in isolation. Our lives and existence are supported by others in seen and unseen ways, be it parents, mentors or society at large. To be aware of these connections, to feel appreciation for them and to strive to give something back to society in a spirit of gratitude is the proper way for human beings to live.'

DAISAKU IKEDA

◆

Attending to Yourself

When you board an airplane, the flight attendants make a safety announcement before take-off. They demonstrate the oxygen masks that automatically drop down in the event of a loss of cabin pressure and they always tell you to put on your own mask before helping others with theirs. This is a great metaphor for life. Before you can give whole-heartedly to a relationship you have to be fit and ready. Connect with yourself little and often in order to maintain a stable emotional state which allows you to receive your partner with love.

Make a date with yourself. Plan it in advance, make the space in your schedule and give everyone around you a 'do not disturb' notice. Use the time to do something that you enjoy like taking a long bath or going for a walk. It doesn't matter what you do, the main things are that you enjoy the activity and it takes you away from your routine.

• Be aware of when you are not operating at peak; give yourself empathy, work out what you need, take your own actions and ask for help.

• Learn to accept help without embarrassment. Allow the giver to enjoy the full sense of giving.

• Throughout the day, just connect with your own breathing for a minute and slow it down.

• Eat healthily, drink water, get enough exercise and sleep.

Perhaps you think you don't have time for any of this? Then you must be suffering on some level. If you're suffering, the relationship will suffer also because your energy is half of that relationship. Right at the beginning of the book we talked about self-responsibility. A relationship might provide refuge but it is not a hospital. You are expected to take the best actions you can to maintain your own well-being and do your own self-healing and self-energizing.

Attending to Your Partner

The best way to attend to your partner is to keep the connection between you alive. If you tend to withdraw or step back, you will need to make an extra effort here. When you keep the connection alive, you become attuned to each other and words diminish in importance as harmony grows and expands.

• Maintain connection by taking turns to listen and speak. This exercise takes 30 minutes and is a good way of starting or ending a week. The person who is the speaker has ten minutes to 'empty out' how they are feeling. The listener gives the speaker two minutes' notice before the ten minutes are up. At the end of the ten minutes the listener takes five minutes to summarize what they heard using the language of feelings and needs. At the end of five minutes the roles are reversed and the exercise repeated.

• Express gratitude with awareness and be consistent. Notice all the things your partner does that contribute to your well-being and consciously give thanks directly to them in a way that they can hear and recognize as gratitude.

• Be interested in what your partner says and does. Even if it is something you didn't like, it is important to explore and understand his or her motivations.

Attending to the Relationship

There is you, your partner and the energy of love that you jointly create and continuously stream. Many couples are just individuals leading parallel lives that intersect with varying degrees of success. There is no real partnership. Doing things together builds mutuality and closeness. When you realize that you are investing in a joint energy stream, you can determine what will give you both the most fulfilment.

Do these things when you have attended to your individual needs and be ready to share in a place where neither of you is in the role of giver or receiver, or listener or speaker. You are both energy channels streaming life into the relationship for the common purpose of making life more wonderful.

• Play and learn together in a non-competitive pursuit. This could be cooking, gardening, crafting or anything else. The aim is to enjoy each other's contribution and work towards an agreed outcome in a spirit of fun.

• Invite beauty into your life. This could be enjoying the arts, the countryside or anything else. The aim is to be together somewhere that is beautiful.

• Find your spiritual identity as a couple. What is your relationship to life and to all of your experiences? One of our most basic spiritual needs is to contribute to each other's and our own well-being. This might be faith based in a traditional religion but it doesn't have to be. It could be as simple as volunteering for a cause that you care about. The aim is to enhance meaning and purpose in your life.

• Do nothing together. Just sit and be. Do nothing in bed, do nothing in nature. Do nothing together, undisturbed.

Attending to Your Environment

Whether you notice it or not, you are affected by your surroundings. It's good to work out which surroundings suit you best, and then create that environment to match your needs. Wherever you live, it is home. Even if you are in temporary accommodation there are simple things you can do to create an atmosphere of harmony and a place where you can relax and enjoy your coupledom. A few simple adjustments can make a world of difference.

• Clear your clutter.
• Add or change colours with flowers, fabrics or objects that you like.
• Allow plants to breathe life into your home if you enjoy looking after them.
• Get comfortable with pillows and cushions.
• Adjust the lighting.
• Control the temperature (as much as you are able) to what is comfortable.

Intimacy & Sex

Sex is the closest and most intimate we can be with each other. It is where the love in a relationship blossoms and shows itself. Of course, sex can just be a physical gratification without any other consideration, but here I am talking about sex as a shared energetic experience, a physical and emotional connection, that we tend to call making love.

When we are in love with our partner, we discover, through lovemaking, pleasures of intimacy that cannot be compared with any other feeling. Experiencing the ecstasy of lying in the arms of the one you love and who loves you reduces any anxieties about how and when you have sex. When we surrender to the pleasures of lovemaking, we merge with our partner as our two energies become one. Making love is a beautiful duet where we can manifest all of the care, recognition, sharing and togetherness that we long for as a direct experience.

Your life is a reflection of your surroundings and a response to it. What you do on the outside will affect what happens to you on the inside. As you become mindful of your surroundings, you will learn to see the external display of your inner chaos and control mechanisms reflected in how you treat your environment.

Roles & Responsibilities

Within the maintenance schedule there are roles and responsibilities. Work out between you who is taking on which role. Using the agreement-making format, use a similar process for agreeing who takes charge of what and how you will make invitations and requests that aren't orders and demands.

Equally, how will you promise to hear a reminder as an invitation and not an order? What is the real conversation and to what language are you both more likely to respond positively? Before we met, David and I had both been in charge of our own businesses and we each complain that the other sounds like a managing director talking to a PA. Old habits die hard and we can see the funny side of looking in the mirror with each other, but some days we do get it dreadfully wrong and a conflict escalates. The beauty of this process is that at any point either one of us (whoever becomes mindful in the moment) can stop the discussion and ask to start again using what we know will work. So that's what we do. It is truly wonderful.

REFLECTIONS

This book is about being mindful in a relationship. I have shown you a path that will awaken you into the present moment. The intention is to build this into your life as a practice. Everything in here can be slotted into a busy life. I am not suggesting you suspend your everyday life; I am suggesting you use some of your time differently.

The purpose is to achieve your goals and enjoy your life right here and now. When you are present, you enjoy everything more because you are focusing with love on the activity you are engaged in at any given moment, and if you don't love it, you change it. When you master this in a relationship the sense of unity is very fulfilling.

Start Again

If this is your first read through the book, I suggest you now go back to the beginning and work through it step by step. Do one thing at a time; do it slowly and deliberately and focus only on the task or activity. Notice what is difficult and how you avoid or resist it and conversely, acknowledge what is easy and how you confront and work through it.

As you become more accomplished at this, you will discover that you both have a better capacity for coping with demanding situations and both feel equipped to make better decisions about your relationship. I wish you well and hope that I have been of service.

A Relationship Contract

Our Contract

This is a living document. We make this contract in a spirit of love and commitment. We give our energy freely to learning and growing in order to keep the relationship alive. From time to time, we agree to review and renegotiate all or parts of this contract to accommodate our individual and joint development. We are entering into this relationship on the following basis:

Unconditional Love

- We have a full understanding of the risks that will be involved.
- We understand that the future has no guarantees and now is the only forever.
- We will be willing to give up unrealistic expectations.
- We understand that our individual fulfilment as human beings will not depend on each other.
- We understand that freedom is something we will give ourselves and we will not belong to each other.
- We will not control each other or make each other do anything.
- We will not have power over each other. We will have power with each other.
- We will hold dear the qualities and traits that brought us together.
- We will acknowledge and value each other as individuals.
- We understand that there will be pain as well as joy and we will share both.
- We will learn from the past but not live in it.
- We will make mutual fun and enjoyment a priority.
- We will maintain enthusiasm for the relationship.

Conditional Agreements

- We will make agreements out of collaboration and dialogue.
- Anything we give to each other will be given voluntarily from the heart and never from obligation.
- We will share equal responsibility for planning and will give our plans the highest priority.
- We will jointly decide our commitments and responsibilities to our roles in the relationship.

- We will make joint agreements about practical issues.
- We will take action to solve problems as soon as they arise.
- We will keep our minds and bodies healthy and will support each other to do so.
- We will make requests of each other and support each other to meet our needs.
- We will never consider ending any of our commitments while angry or upset.
- If one of us begins to feel differently about the relationship, we agree a 'change of heart' period of one year during which time we will explore our future.
- Even if we should part, we will commit to keeping all the confidences shared between us.

Trust
- We will be reliable.
- We won't say that we'll do anything unless we truly want to do it and actually will.
- We will not lie to each other by word or action or by failure to share relevant information that affects our relationship.
- We will be strong for one another when one or both of us are feeling weak.
- We will not discreetly or overtly give sexual signals to others. We will count on each other to recognize and admire our sexuality and attractiveness.
- We will respect, accept and appreciate if one of us says no and be genuinely interested in the reasons.
- When one of us says no, we will willingly explore the reasons together.
- We will accept anger, sadness, upset and fear without attempting to control each other's feelings.
- No matter how angry or upset one of us feels, we will never threaten or harm each other physically.
- We won't get so caught up in our own stuff that we ignore each other.
- We will not unexpectedly withdraw before, during or after any shared activities that we have planned.
- We won't ridicule each other or use shared confidences against each other.
- We will make time for being together for dialogue, work, play and love.
- We will value and protect sexual expression in our relationship as a time and place for intimacy.

INDEX

agreements 8, 66, 121–4
  conditional 122, 140–1
  unspoken contracts 91–3
analytical ability 61
assumptions 30

Baker, Paul 64
blame 15, 17, 18, 19, 48
Bulwer-Lytton, Edward 106

children 73, 111
collage 44
communication 37–8, 52, 73
  see also dialogue; engagement
compassionate honesty 36
conditional agreements 122, 140–1
conflict management 60
Confucius 61
contentment 46, 89–90
coping strategies 85–8

Dalai Lama 99
debate 101–3, 104
dialogue 71–3
  authenticity 100–1, 103
  closing a session 78–9
  conditions for 105–8
  debate and 101–3, 104
  definition 101
  exploring the past 111–13
  guidelines for 115–17
  hopes, fears & dreams 114–17
  listening 60–2, 74, 75–8, 79,
    116, 134
  preparing for 71–3
  questions 73–9
  repeating 74, 75–8, 116

  space for 107–8
  see also engagement
dreams 114–17

emotional baggage 17
emotional punishment 40–1
emotional support 37–8
emotional vulnerability 105
empathy 76–8
engagement 62, 117
  conditions for 65–70
  permission to engage 66–7
  preparing for 63–4
  refusal to engage 69
  time to talk 68–9, 106
  see also dialogue
escalating situations 28–30

facilitation 60
fears 41, 114–17
feelings 23–4, 48, 49–50
  language of 87
  processing 49
flexibility 8, 61, 94
forgiveness 54–6, 63
free yourself 56

Gandhi, Mahatma 40
garden of contentment 44–6, 47–8,
  52, 53, 70
genuineness 61
guided visioning 47–8
guilt 41, 46
gut instinct 100–1

Ikeda, Daisaku 132
inner truth 103–8

INDEX

internal police officer 41
interpretations 30
intimacy 32, 69, 94, 137

judging 15, 16, 48

learning from experience 61
letting go 111
listening 60–2, 74, 75–8, 79,
    116, 134
lying 39–42

Mandela, Nelson 56
Maslow, Abraham 90
Max-Neef, Manfred 31–2
mediation 52–3, 69
mindfulness 10–11, 42–3, 79
mistakes
    admitting past mistakes 112–13
    learning from 113
motivating factors 41–2

needs
    compromise or change 88–93, 94
    exploring 90–1
    fundamental 31–2
    language of 87
    physical 45
    reluctance and 50–2
    social 45
    spiritual 45
    unmet 85

openness to other people 61

perception checking 28–30
position 21–2, 28, 29, 93

power imbalance 108–9
power struggles 94
pretending 39
punishment 18, 19, 38, 40–1

quality of life 42–3

rapport building 60
relationship contract 140–1
reluctance 50–2
resentment 46, 55, 56, 63
resistance to change 18, 20,
    63–4, 100
Rilke, Rainer Maria 83
roles & responsibilities 138
Rosenberg, Marshall 6, 49, 65
Rumi 37

safety 65, 108–11
self-acceptance 52–3
self-awareness 61
self-healing & self-energizing
    exercise 25–8, 53, 71, 126–9
self-knowing 47–8
self-suppression 36–8, 43
self-understanding 47–8
sex 105, 137
shame 41, 46, 56
starting point for change 14–7, 32
strategies 120–6

trust 65, 69, 109, 114, 122, 141

unconditional love 122, 140
unspoken contracts 91–3

vulnerability 103, 105

OTHER BOOKS IN THE MINDFULNESS SERIES

**The Art of Mindful
Gardening**

ISBN: 978-1-907332-59-3

**The Art of Mindful
Walking**

ISBN: 978-1-907332-58-6

**Happiness and
How it Happens**

ISBN: 978-1-907332-93-7

**Meditation and the
Art of Beekeeping**

ISBN: 978-1-907332-39-5

**Mindfulness & the Art
of Managing Anger**

ISBN: 978-1-908005-30-4

**The Mindfulness
Budget**

ISBN: 978-1-907332-41-8

**The Mindfulness
Diet**

ISBN: 978-1-907332-40-1

**Seeking Silence
in a Noisy World**

ISBN: 978-1-908005-11-3

**Zen and the Art of
Raising Chickens**

ISBN: 978-1-907332-38-8